The Teachings of Vimala Thakar

The Teachings of
Vimala Thakar

CHRISTINE TOWNEND

Edited and Translated by
JACK GONTIER

MOTILAL BANARSIDASS PUBLISHERS
PRIVATE LIMITED • DELHI

First Edition: Delhi, 2010
First published in French by Le Lotus d'Or *in 2006,*
titled L'Enseignement de Vimala Thakar

ISBN: 978-81-208-3335-7

MOTILAL BANARSIDASS

41 U.A. Bungalow Road, Jawahar Nagar, Delhi 110007
8 Mahalaxmi Chamber, 22 Bhulabhai Desai Road, Mumbai 400026
203 Royapettah High Road, Mylapore, Chennai 600004
236, 9th Main III Block, Jayanagar, Bangalore 560011
Sanas Plaza, 1302 Baji Rao Road, Pune 411002
8 Camac Street, Kolkata 700017
Ashok Rajpath, Patna 800004
Chowk, Varanasi 221001

Printed in India

By Jainendra Prakash Jain at Shri Jainendra Press,
A-45 Naraina, Phase-I, New Delhi 110028
and published by Narendra Prakash Jain for
Motilal Banarsidass Publishers Private Limited,
Bungalow Road, Delhi 110007

This book is dedicated to
MR. JACK GONTIER,
whose publishing company,
Le Lotus d'Or, has been instrumental
in making available
Vimala Thakar's teaching to French readers.

A radical mutation in the quality of human consciousness will take place. We are concerned with preparing the ground for the emergence of a new human race.

Without false modesty Vimalaji can claim that the source of Ultimate Reality is no more a theory or an abstraction for her. She lives in the Divinity that has been fathomed, but Vimala has not initiated anyone according to the Indian tradition, therefore she says, "I am not a Guru."

— *Vimala Thakar*

CONTENTS

INTRODUCTION

Vimalaji's life has been dedicated to the work of giving a modern presentation of the great and eternal truths of the Ancient Wisdom in the belief that eventually that Reality will be given preeminence in daily living, and our world will become a paradise where humans and animals and forests and flowers are revered instead of plundered, and the word 'love' is not something corny and embarrassing, but becomes the accepted, underlying principle of all human interactions and activities.

Vimalaji sometimes said that her Teaching is a modern interpretation of Raja Yoga, a system expounded by the sage Patanjali in his *Yoga Sutras* (553 B.C.). It is the 'path of understanding', in which all levels and layers of the being, body, emotions, mind, and psyche are purified by self-education or spiritual enquiry. I use the word 'Teaching' with a capital 'T' to denote the fact that it is an inclusive component of a body of spiritual wisdom (not particular to any religion) which has been taught by many realized beings throughout the ages, from the time the Vedas and Upanishads were issued forth by the Himalayan Masters. Vimalaji acknowledged she communicated with, as They exist in etheric form.

When it was first suggested to me that I should study Vimalaji's books, I felt disappointed that they seemed to contain a lot of generalised words and platitudes. It was some years later, when I again returned to the books, that I realised I had misunderstood Vimalaji's use of 'code words'. To give one example: if you look up the abstract noun 'silence' in the Oxford dictionary, you see it means 'absence of sound, abstinence from speech'. But when Vimalaji is speaking of 'silence' it means something much greater, much more profound and far-reaching than this tight, dictionary definition: it describes a particular state of consciousness.

There are many other words which may sound abstracted and generalised on a first reading, and therefore, being too broad, create a difficulty in comprehension. But in fact each of these words has a specific meaning in her Teaching – *Wholeness, Intelligence, Inner Revolution, Dimension, Desire, Life, Individual, Ego–* to name but a few. It seems that there is a purpose in these words being used with a veil of generality. It means that the reader has to search beneath the surface dictionary meaning to find his or her own understanding of the code word, thus resulting in true enquiry, with no easy answers, no immediate solutions, but rather many statements which need cogitation and examination, then leading to small revelations and thereby graded and gradual expansions of understanding.

Essentially Vimalaji's Teaching could be perceived to have two non-divisible, interconnected aspects : firstly, that which examines the origin, meaning, purpose and destiny of this universe, humanity's place within it and relationship to the natural world; and secondly, a means by which one can realise for oneself one's true nature, the 'inner revolution' which is a result of the passionate quest for self-realisation. It brings about 'total transformation' in the multi-dimensional human being, who represents a portion of 'condensed cosmos', an individuated unit of the Divinity which is indivisible from the Whole.

Vimalaji's Teachings were for me a confirmation of sanity; I found that my own inquiry, my own experiences, my own discoveries, were not mad imaginings, not hallucinations and ecstatic visions, but a common experience which so many humans have undergone. So I knew that I was not deranged, but indeed normal. It was, in fact, those who had never made any inquiry into the functions of consciousness who were abnormal, for they were seeing the world through these jelly human eyes instead of through the field of radiant, individuated consciousness, which has mistakenly identified itself as a human ego.

At a certain moment, whilst putting together the compilation, I began to have doubts as to whether I was in any position to undertake such a project, and whether it was merely presumption on my part to assume I could fulfill such a task. I informed Vimalaji about my feelings and she wrote the following in reply: 'Dear Christine, Your hesitation …is out of place. You are an authority by yourself and have every right to communicate your understanding of the teachings of any Teacher.'

The outside world of events and phenomena is only a covering and a veiling of the all-permeating, ever-existing Reality, which is unseen and unrecognized by human eyes but forever present, and I wished to share this understanding. I am therefore grateful that Vimalaji has allowed me to fulfill this wish, to become the guide who is introducing the reader to the wonderment and miracle and magic of the Teaching of a modern Master.

There are now over sixty publications containing transcriptions from recorded talks given by Vimalaji to various groups in various countries over the past few decades, and other publications containing various writings by Vimalaji. I chose many of the quotations from sources which have not been widely distributed, especially the magazine, *The Invincible*, which is no longer produced. At the beginning of each chapter of this compilation I have written a short introduction. I have also included a glossary. I feel compelled to constantly express the limitations of the English language in describing things which are beyond conceptualization, that are vast and great and awe-inspiring, and way beyond the limitations of the human mind and speech .

VIMALA THAKAR
A Life Sketch

I belong to no country though I was born in India.
I feel I belong to the whole of humanity.[1]

The life of Vimalaji was not an ordinary life. It was the life of a person who had given all of herself, fully and completely, to fulfill whatever the 'Cosmic Movement' caused to happen in and around her. There is not a word she taught which she had not understood, which she had not herself experienced through facing challenges in which she risked her life personally for the causes in which she believed, and which she promoted, and through the personal inner *sadhana*, which was already completed and understood from the moment of her birth.

On a material level, she was involved with some of the great Indian leaders of the 20th century who fought for independence from Britain, and for democracy in the village. But on another level, she came to do something even more important, one could almost say, private, a gift to the world not yet fully recognised – re-presentation, a re-purification of the ancient Vedic and Upanishadic Teaching, which had become polluted through centuries of degradation, mis-interpretation and misunderstanding.

In a manner which could be said to be miraculous, Vimalaji had gone back to the source of the major scriptures, communicating outside time and space with the Rishis who first spoke these Teachings, and presented a pure and exact interpretation based on exact translation of the Sanskrit words and their original meaning in the context of spiritual understanding.

Vimala Thakar (Vimalaji) was born on the 15th April 1925, in the state of Maharashtra (India). As a child she was clairvoyant, and realised beings came to visit her parents on several occasions to point out that she did not belong to the parents, she belonged to the world. As a very young child (age six) she went wandering into the forest to search for 'God' as a family friend had told her she would find God in the forest. She said about her early days:

'At the age of three she had started to look for God, and it was that which had led her wandering off into the forest, where she thought she could find God. From the age of seven she had trained herself to sit for fourteen hours at a time, and at the age of fourteen she sat for seventy-two hours at a stretch. She had gone into samadhi during one of these sittings, and her parents had needed to call a yogi known to the family in order to bring her back to body consciousness.'[2]

After she finished her Masters Degree (on Western and Eastern philosophy), she had a 'very deep yearning' to go to the Himalayas and she spent about three months in a cave near Rishikesh, which Swami Ramtirth had once occupied. During this period of intense spiritual practice she grew thin and debilitated, eating only mangoes and vegetables which she cooked in a pit, and drinking the polluted water of the Ganges. Indeed, she grew so weak she fell into the Ganges while she was washing one day, and was rescued by some devotees of Swami Shivananda. Later she was to say that she learnt from this experience that to live in isolation for long periods is not an efficacious means of practicing *sadhana* and does not bring real peace.

In 1953 Vimalaji met Vinoba Bhave (1895-1982), founder and leader of the Land Gift Movement in India, and one of Gandhiji's most famous disciples. He offered her the opportunity to join the campaign in which the Bhoodan movement requested wealthy landholders to give some of their estates to the landless labourers who worked on them. Vimalaji was interested in socialism, and keen to join this movement, as she believed that 'life was for living' and that evolution of the human psyche could only take place when confronted by the daily challenges of life. Nonetheless she said to Vinoba Bhave, 'I will give you some of my time, not all of my time,' meaning that she wished there was to be balance in her life, combining active service with periods of withdrawal.

Vimalaji worked for the Bhoodan Movement for eight years. It was during her work for the land gift movement that she met Krishnamurti in 1956. When Krishnamurti asked her 'Why are you working?', she replied, 'Because through it [the Bhoodan Movement] I can express myself, my love for human beings.' 'Not to help them?' Krishnamurti asked her. 'Who am I to help others, sir?' she replied to him. Indeed, in later years, Vimalaji was often to say that it was the person who performed the social action who was the one to benefit by it, and that therefore one should never be proud or boastful about 'helping' others.

In 1959 Vimala met with a serious car accident in the hills of Assam. Miraculously her life was saved, but as she was thrown from the jeep she was hurtled down a cliff and fell against a tree, smashing the side of her head. One ear was badly damaged. It continued to bleed and became infected, causing fever and pain. Despite visits to the best doctors, both in India and abroad, the ear did not heal, and Vimalaji said she was prepared for death at this time. It was Krishnamurti who made the suggestion to her that he could perhaps try to heal the ear. Thus she underwent several healing sessions with Krishnaji, and the ear as restored to normal functioning.

In 1961, Vimalaji was invited by Krishnamurti to come to Saanen (Switzerland), where she listened to his talks. As she traveled in Europe, she made friends with many of Krishnaji's followers. These people, recognising the strange, peaceful, Buddha-like appearance of the young woman, began to ask her questions about Krishnamurti's teachings, to which she would respond. Soon she was mixing with the rich and famous of Europe. She was encouraged by Krishnamurti to start speaking and despite her reticence she spoke to those who had requested it, although she would not allow herself to be called a teacher. She felt it necessary, for the sake of clarification, to explain to people that she was not speaking on behalf of Krishnamurti, she was speaking on behalf of herself. But it was her attention to integrity that was to cause the rift, apparently generated by those around Krishnamurti. This is how Vimalaji described the events:

> The publication of 'The Flame of Life' and 'The Eloquence of Ecstasy' had been widely criticized... Some accused me of repeating Krishnamurti's verses. The word 'plagiarism' was used later on in connection with talks given in Holland in 1964. Publication of those talks... seems to have disturbed many a person. Some of those who knew my intimate association with J. Krishnamurti felt hurt that I never mentioned his contribution to my life in my talks. Some felt hurt that instead of propagating Krishnamurti's teachings, I dared to give independent talks. Some felt annoyed that I dared to print those talks. This made my heart rather sad. In great agony I wrote to one of my friends on the 18th February, 1966:
>
> ... 'I have never claimed to be Krishnamurti's disciple I am an insignificant human being –one of the billions living on this globe. But I have my life to live. I am contented in living it. I have no time for carrying on anybody else's mission. And who says Krishnamurti has a mission independent of, and different from living?'[3]

There were certain points in her own understanding of Life which did not exactly coincide with those of Krishnaji. Vimalaji had mentioned in one of her books that she saw the truth differently from Krishnaji in one small aspect :

*We have in the world two categories – those who
convert the techniques and methods into rituals and
make them empty repetition, and those who throw
away the conditions or the methods and techniques
without having touched the truth, the essence as
fact in their life. You can either throw away the
discipline or you can understand the importance
of it.*

*J. Krishnamurti has tried to take humanity to the
level of : Listen, understand, act instantaneously
and be transformed, and I find that transformation
cannot take place unless the biological system is
cleansed. So, sitting in silence is for purification,
for cleansing, for merging oneself into the ocean of
silence, of non-motion. But a person who reads
Krishnamurti's books would say: "Why should you
sit in silence day after day? If you sit day after day
it's a discipline, it's repeating." You take meals every
day, does that become repetitive? You also sleep
every night; is sleeping a repetitive, mechanistic
activity? Is your breathing a repetitive thing for you?
Why should plunging into the state of non-action,
non-motion, plunging into the state of thought-free
consciousness, become a repetitive or mechanistic
thing? Unless you merge your psychological system
also into the state of non-action and non-movement
you cannot be back in the wholeness of your being.[4]*

Vimalaji had resolved that she did not want publicity, did not
want fame, did not want large audiences, but wanted to teach in
the tradition of the Vedas, with small groups of friends, so that
an intimate exchange could take place, and real spiritual
upliftment could occur, rather than with halls of individuals,
gathered as much out of emotionalism and curiosity as out of a
real spirit of inquiry.

> *The sensitivity of love does not allow me to assert or preach. I don't want to convince anyone, to convert anyone. Sharing in friendship is something very beautiful. You sit on the footing of equality and you share. If I have the motive to convince you, to convert you, to propound, to propagate, then it will be a very subtle kind of violence committed against you.*[5]

Throughout the following years Vimalaji's teaching continued to expand with journeys to many parts of the world, particularly in Holland, Italy, Norway, Chile, and the USA. The constant travel must have been exhausting and finally, in 1990 she decided not to travel any more. Groups of students from Europe now came to hear her speak either in Mt. Abu or Dalhousie, where she spent the summers. Some profound teachings and publications were the result of these small groups. We have to admit, though, that, for the large part, her life has passed unheralded and unnoticed by the world. And sometimes I feel regret that the profound truths which she has spoken, born of so much love and meditation, born of the Brahman Itself, have not as yet found the recognition which they deserve.

> *I spend practically and hour and a half with the Rishi every morning between 3 and 4.30, sometimes 3.30 to 5.00, just to be with them, in order to feel the spirit behind their words. It is quite a responsibility to bring to the 20th century what was conceived and pronounced thousands of years back. You have to travel back thousands of years.*[6]
>
> *Bringing the Energy into expression is done by becoming a small instrument. It's very necessary to empty yourself so you don't have any purpose and then, when the Cosmic works through you, the Cosmic gets fulfilled. It does require to be totally empty in order to be filled with the Cosmic. The event of Vimala's life is like a flute being played by Krishna. The divinity plays its own music.*

Those with sensitivity and perception who entered into a room where Vimalaji sat, became aware of a sense of Presence, not of any individual consciousness, but of a vast spread of consciousness which seems to contain all the Energy and Love of the universe.

Realisation

The inner journey that my consciousness was taking was leading me very fast towards a crisis. I had started doubting the propriety of my being associated with any organised revolutionary movement. If revolution was entirely a voyage into the Unknown, if it was concerned with creating a new mind, how could I continue to represent unorganised thought? How could I preach an ideology?[7]

I wrote to my father on 15 August 1961:
'Everything has dropped away. A tremendous tempest has swept away everything with one stroke... an intense flame of passion is consuming the whole being... I wish I could describe how I witnessed the ego being torn to pieces and being thrown to the winds. I wish I could communicate what this denudation is! Or may one call it excentration? The centre of thinking getting dissolved into nothingness.'[8]

On 16th July, 1962, in Saanen, when she was sitting in the garden alone, on this bright and sunny day, Vimalaji says: 'A moment occurred [where] the solitude became so intact that I did not need to be alone any more'. When asked if this was the first time a person knows *samadhi,* at the moment of liberation, she replied:

Perhaps you could call that moment the last flimsy curtain being removed; the last influence of personality ceased, and it was as if a curtain was drawn –I mean, moved aside. The last sense of duality was gone.[9]

Vimalaji further commented on this period of her life:

I remember a day in Benares in October or November, 1962. I walked up to see Krishnaji who was at his residence in Benares and said, 'Krishnaji, what has happened that I am so denuded? I don't have a sense of belonging.' He took my hand and he led me up a path along the veranda to a rose which was half-opened and he asked me, 'Where does this flower belong?' Then he continued, 'It belongs to the space, and space carries the flowering. Why must you belong anywhere?' So it was like this. There's no final moment. Even today I don't feel I've arrived – the nuances and shades of reality go on opening up every moment

so mutation is a dynamic, infinite process which would go on until the cosmic evolution exhausts all the potential contained in its Wholeness.[10]

The structure of 'me-ness' has collapsed. The roof of 'my-ness' has blown away. The foundation of knowledge has been broken. The walls of principles have been shattered. The ideals of ideology have fallen apart. The whole of 'me' is looted... In the looting away of all that was 'mine' has been the death of the 'me'... Now who shall make claim to immortality?... I myself am lost. There is nothing left to remain as remnants. Thus what now is, is nothing![11]

There happened a marvel. In between two thoughts the beauty of sheer nothingness shone.[12]

PART ONE

MAN AND THE UNIVERSE

1. MACROCOSM AND MICROCOSM

The levels and layers, the interpenetrating dimensions of the Absolute as it shines forth and expresses itself in the multiplicity of matter, the energy fields which spread through time and space and universes, these levels and layers of Existence are One, they are an 'homogenous Wholeness'. We could perhaps imagine our Cosmos as originating from a Vast Endless Blackness, an 'Absolute Ground of Existence' beyond space and time, and from this huge Energy Source, issues forth the gales of electrical will or 'desire' or 'love' which bring the dispersed and scattered gases and matter into a coherent physical, phenomenal world. Each layer of Energy, each sheet of dazzle, becomes denser and slower moving as it materialises and finally concretises as physical matter which we can see with our physical eyes.

But beyond our physical eyes and physical senses lie so many other fields of energy as yet unperceived by us. In these higher, rarer, fields there is no concept of time and space, no concept of the petty, human thoughts and greeds which consume us. There is only an unmoving, relentlessly adoring consciousness which is Love and Completion, and which knows no imperfection. Behind this consciousness there is the Black Void Depth of the Absolute Ground of Existence which we cannot know, and from which the Universal Consciousness has emerged (and is inseparably part of) and engendered the phenomenal world. In the Ancient Wisdom this has been described as Prakash (or Purusha) and Prakriti, Purusha being the Absolute Void which permeates and interpenetrates and supports and gives life to the play of Prakriti, the spinning, colliding atoms and genes of physical life, including the mind in all its levels both fine and grosser, and emotions, the ego and its content.

Vimalaji stated that humans beings are 'condensed cosmos, there is no qualitative difference between the microcosm and the macrocosm, as regards the essence'. I believe it is for this reason that she said there is no individual soul, or psyche or Atman, but she has also talked about 'individuated' consciousness, meaning that in the endless Fields of the universal Essence or Energy, on the different 'planes', there are immersed individuated fields, each with its own ring-pass-not.

The soul is a small spark of the infinite Soul, Paramatman. If we look at the world as a soul rather than through human eyes, then we see the same visual images but with a cc :pletely different understanding, because a different 'organ' is perceiving. Nonetheless, the soul, psyche or Atma is itself continually refining the vibratory energies of its force-field and therefore also constitutes something impermanent and changeable. The soul is the harbinger of the 'Presence', the Absolute. It is through the transformation of the soul, through its love, its sacrifice, that we are put in touch with our true Self, which is the indivisible Spark, the Monad, the Void. Thus it is through and because of 'the total revolution' that the human mind becomes a direct reflector of the Spirit, the Father, the Absolute. Therefore, the soul-form is defined as part of the Prakriti, the play of matter, whereas the Source, the original Point within the nothingness, the ISNESS, is the Purusha.

The human monad, or Atman, or individuated Absolute Ground of Existence, could be said to be the 'eye' of the Absolute, through which that great Life can sense the play of matter, the Lila, the dance of existence, which issues forth and is again withdrawn in the vast cycles of universes and the small cycles of humans, animals and vegetation.

Vimalaji stated that the great revolutionary Teaching of the Buddha was that He was able to divulge to humanity the non-existence of Atman, anatma, and 'by that term, he was referring to the non-existence of "I" as a separate entity, as a permanent entity.' He was able to see that the ego, the personality, was an invention of the mind, a temporary, passing collection of *dancing molecules and atoms and electrons, but it was not the Reality. Therefore we can conclude that there are great Entities who are individuated radiance, who have attained samadhi, who express Themselves directly through the centreless point, or Monad, or Absolute which has become Their Being. Such Rishis, or sages, or Masters, remain accessible to those who are themselves aware in such a dimension. In her teaching and conversations, Vimalaji not infrequently, referred to her contact and communication with such Beings.*

There is only consciousness, either *nispanda* (without vibrations) or *spanda* (with vibrations).[1] When the consciousness vibrates, the *spanda* creates the duality of the subject and object, the duality of individual consciousness and the cosmic consciousness. So this seems to be the basic ignorance... having roots in our minds, in our consciousness.[2]

Awareness is the movement of the universal consciousness, the supramental consciousness, the cosmic consciousness or the supreme Intelligence as Krishnamurthi would call it. The supreme Intelligence, Brahman of the Vedanta, Chiti of Yoga, Shiva of the Bhakti Yoga, they are different names given to the same. And when there is movement of that universal consciousness in human beings, you call it awareness. Awareness is the effect of that movement.[3]

It seems to me that the name 'awareness' is given to that energy which does not require a subject like the 'I', the 'me' the ego, which is not limited by any circumference or periphery of human knowledge and experience or inheritance, which is all-inclusive. It does not require the relationship of subject and object. It is an all-inclusive attentivity, nonobjective and non-subjective... So awareness is an energy qualitatively different from the energy of thought, of impulses of instincts, etc.[4]

The cosmos is a great thought of the [space-time] continuum, which crystallises as stars, planets and other physical bodies. Each galaxy appears to be a lonely lighthouse in the continuum; each star appears to be a tiny lamp in the galaxy; each planet appears to be a remnant of a tiny lamp when it is put off. Each habitable planet is a zoo containing inanimate and living organisms... There are billions and billions of such zoos in the cosmos... The cosmic mind constructs the spacetime continuum. The physical cosmos, the manifest, is a great thought of the cosmic mind.[5]

...after a life-long study of the Vedas and the Upanishads, the oriental and the occidental philosophies, it seems to me that the whole cosmos, *Brahmanand*, is a field of, or is the interaction and dance of innumerable energies. It is the interaction of energies that creates what you call matter of material objects. Matter is nothing but the solidification of energies which are nebulous, fluid, which have vibrational existence. As this is true in the case of cosmos it is true in the case of our bodies, the physical bodies that you and I have: we are fields for the interaction of very many energies – some are known to us and many are still unknown to us. [6]

[The body] is an expression of cosmic life. What we call 'our body' is condensed cosmos. All that which exists is cosmos, all the energies existing and operating in the cosmos are operating in what you call this physical organism. It is a conditioned and condensed form of the cosmic life, because the Intelligence has its abode in this body.[7] Human beings are condensed cosmos, there is no qualitative difference between the microcosm and the macrocosm, as regards the essence.[8] When you realize that the Atman and the Brahman, the essence of your life and the essence of cosmos, are one and the same in quality, then there is no sense of identification, there is no need for identification, there is no need to say 'I am one with That', there is no need even to say 'I am That.' [9]

Why should Life have a 'human meaning'? Its spontaneousness is meaning-free. Its existence does not depend upon the human brain and its concepts or ideas. Life is sacred just because human brain has not played any part in its generation. It is a self-generated Creativity which knows not destruction or death.[10]

Life (you may call it cosmos) is self-generated. There is not a creator or a personal god who created the world and remained outside of it. It is a self-generated, self-controlled, self-regulated phenomenon. Life seems to be an Intelligence, an energy of Intelligence which has been unwinding, uncovering, manifesting itself for millions and millions of years and yet has remained ever virgin and ever fresh... Life is an infinite and eternal phenomenon... an expression of eternal Intelligence.[11]

The whole Life is divine, the whole Life is Divinity. It is a dance of emergence and merging back; it is a dance of manifestation and dissolution; it is a beginningless and endless dance of so many energies. I do not recognise any God apart from the Cosmic Life. One is aware that there is not the creator and the creation relationship; but there is an all-permeating energy of Intelligence, ever uncovering itself. [12]

Life is the cosmic dance of formlessness manifesting itself into innumerable patterns of forms, and the forms having played around and in space of nothingness merge back into the formlessness from where they had come. The formlessness, the nothingness, the emptiness of space, seems to be creativity; that creativity is called Being or Beingness.[13]

The cycle of life goes on, universes are created and universes merge back, species are generated, species merge back. Like the ripples on the water they are generated and they merge back into the water. As the rays of the sun merge back into the sun, so also the species emerge out of matter, and merge back when their potential is exhausted.[14]

Life is an eternity, there are no moments in Life and no hours in Life. This is only our calculation, this is our measurement used for our convenience. Life is time-free ISNESS. You may call it eternity, infinity, immeasurable, unnamable, etc. You may use any words. It is an Isness. Now it gets focused at the crossing of space and time in your physical life.[15]

WHOLENESS OF LIFE

This organic Being, the wholeness where everything is inter-related, this Being explodes into becoming and yet the process of becoming does not affect the inexhaustibility, the virginity and the majesty of the Being... Every exploded expression shares the creative energy and yet the Wholeness does not become incomplete, nothing is detracted out of the Beingness of the Isness or the wholeness.[16]

The homogeneous Wholeness of Life has dynamism and that dynamism expresses itself in the explosion or emergence of innumerable energies. In the process of becoming, the nothingness (nothingness) of Life, the nobody-ness (nobodyness) of Life which is called Emptiness, is exploding into innumerable forms and expressions. The very variety of those forms, shapes, tastes, perfumes is staggering. And in spite of that inexhaustible variety of manifestations, expressions or explosions, the ISNESS of Life remains whole, nothing is detracted from its wholeness.[17]

Life is an organic Wholeness, it is not an artificially structured totality, it is not an abstraction created by philosophers, it is a living Being. Life is a wholeness having the quality of Beingness, of Isness. The one has not become many, creating a dichotomy between the One and the many. The Oneness has exploded into manyness. It is not One against the many. The Oneness and the explosion of the Oneness cause the emergence of manyness. After all, the words 'one' and 'many' are creations of the human mind. As long as you say 'the One has become the many' you look upon the One as the creator and the many as creation. *There is neither the creator nor the creation.* There is only a wholeness of Life emerging into the manyness and the manyness merging back into the Oneness.[18]

___

The energy of Life is a perceptive* Intelligence. Life is Isness and Energy, both. All these together constitute the Wholeness, the organic Wholeness of life. [19]

___

The Cosmic Energies have their own way of functioning.There is an interrelatedness, a magnificent orderliness, a majestic harmony among all the energies, maintaining their identity without disturbing the homogeneous unity or oneness of Life, that is the Cosmic Life. If you would like to call all this as the cosmic laws or principles, you may so call them. We are related to them. We have the responsibility to live that relationship, to discharge our responsibility of contributing to that harmony, contributing to that orderliness or at least not to disturb the innate organic orderliness and harmony which seems to be the principle of Life. In human terminology, you may call it love and compassion.[20]

___

Life cannot be divided into individual and collective, the inner and the outer, the physical and the psychological ; it is one indivisible whole. The substratum of life is a continuum of unconditioned all-conscious energy, which is eternal and immutable. It is homogeneous, undifferentiated and dimensionless... each infinitesimal point in the continuum has the same nature as the continuum itself... The Unity (the Continuum, the Void) has an infinite creative potential. The Void is

___

*In this context 'perceptive Intelligence' means the Cosmic Movement, the Universal Consciousnessness which is the second aspect, or emitted, moving Energy, the dazzle, the Love, the electro-magnetic extension, which has been brought into activity as an expression of the ISNESS or Absolute unmoving Ground of Existence.

the non-vibrating, unconditioned universal Consciousness. In the language of modern physics, the Void is called the Field. The Field is the only reality. The Field is the absolute space. The Field is the living Void, which manifests as creation and the creation then dissolves into the Field. So the Field has a dynamic nature. The Field, the Void is fullness; it is the wholeness of life.[21]

You will not be able to measure this omnipotent and omnipresent energy of Intelligence permeating Life everywhere. Divinity is immeasurable. It is a mystery that can be felt. On the visible level, you feel with the senses, in the invisible you feel with the mind or the brain with the help of words. And then in the infinite or eternal, the mysterious can be felt with your whole being. It is a wholeness, so it has to be related to the wholeness of your being. That for me is religion: living simultaneously with the visible, the invisible and the Infinite.[22]

Every system [in the physical body] is autonomous, independent, and yet they are interrelated organically, so they make one whole. It is a functioning of many creative energies operating through very many organs and yet making a harmonious whole. It is a wholeness like the cosmos, it is a wholeness having innumerable energies; some are conditioned and some are not conditioned.[23]

Look at this discovery made thousands of years ago ! These people [sages, rishis] through their investigation, their experimentations on their body, they arrived at this Truth. This basic Truth that we have to learn and incorporate in our way of living, that the whole cosmos is an organism. The planet earth is a living organism vibrating with Life. Life permeates every body; Life permeates everything. Do not call the earth a thing; do not call a tree, a mountain or river a thing. They are Beings. The whole cosmos is a living organism and it has parts like the human body has parts. The trees, the mountains, the oceans, the rivers, the animals and human beings – they are all inter-related in a very intelligent way.[24]

Life is one, indivisible, homogeneous wholeness, it cannot be divided, it cannot be compartmentalized, it cannot be fragmented. The value sense in human consciousness is derived from the awareness of this complex wholeness, from the awareness of the homogeneity and complexity of the wholeness simultaneously. What does that mean? It means that in this Cosmos every expression of life is inter-related to every other expression of life. There is inter-relatedness and inter-dependence of all expressions of life. If earth is one expression of life, the space of the skies is another, the streams of water another. All these expressions of life, along with the nonhuman and human species are biologically inter-related.[25]

In Life 'things' do not exist, but whatever exists is a being. The earth is a being, the galaxies are beings, the oceans, the mountains are all beings. What does that mean? It means that they are intelligent companions of the human race. You cannot talk even of a particle of matter as a thing, because it contains a quantum of energy defying human mathematics or logic; it has its own energy of Intelligence.[26]

❖ ❖ ❖ ❖ ❖ ❖

2. LOVE AND DESIRE

LOVE

For the emanation of the razor sharp energy of Love, that perceives without the perceiver, and responds without the centre, this wiping out of all that we have posited, all that the human race has posited, is essential... Would you allow the movement of inquiry, which is the movement of psychological knowledge, to end and let there be that naked silence, that naked emptiness? To be filled with that silence, to be filled with the nothingness of that emptiness, is an adventure.[1]

To Vimalaji love was inseparale from self-realisation. The Word 'love' did not refer to the possessive, conditioned love which goes under that name, the 'love' which makes a woman cling onto her children after they are independent, the love which selects one person as an object of affection, and another as an object of dislike. This love is the distorted tainting of the real Love which is a consistent, persisting, never-changing, never-modified, pouring forth which forever remains pure and untrammeled despite the corruptions and distortions which might be imposed upon it by human interpretations and twistings. The real Love (with a capital 'L') is inseparable from the One Unicity, IS indeed the One Unicity, the universal consciousness of which every soul is an inseparable part, the emanation from The One About Whom Naught Can be Said, the Absolute, the Monad.

Why is this 'Love' razor sharp? 'Razor sharp' represents a purity, an uncluttered penetrating directedness, without any obstruction, a direct, immediate, acute perception. How does it 'perceive without the perceiver'? In the state of samadhi, there is no observing point, there is only an endless Void expansion in which the Energy of Love is integrally incorporated.

How does it 'respond without the centre?' There is no person thinking 'I am observing'. On the contrary, the person is part of the outside, part of the external, distant visible world and the ITNESS looks through the person.

What is 'this wiping out of all that we have posited?' We had imagined, created, cluttered a stream of records and images on strips through time, and all of this is shredded, dissolved, in the absolute state of Beingness, of Itness.

What is the 'ending of psychological knowledge?' There is an ending even of a sense of the inhabiting Presence, the Witness which has for eons been the infinite Observing Angel. It ends when the soul itself merges into the Infinite Monad, the Absolute, the Void, the 'naked silence, the naked emptiness'. This is true samadhi, beyond even the movement of Love, the movement of the undivided, infinite, all-pervading Isness or One Unicity.

What is 'that naked silence, that naked emptiness'? That naked emptiness, is the vaccuumless, devoid, centrifugal, black of nothing filled with everything, including the Energies of Love and Desire (Will).

In the state of Silence one is able to feel the One Unicity, the 'Homogenous Wholeness of Life' the 'Isness of life'. This is Love itself, pure, 'razor-sharp', 'responding without a centre,' The person in the state of silence, or observation, feels in all levels and layers of the being, the Energy of an Infinite, allpervading, Love (which I have termed the One Unicity because there are no words to describe It). This Energy is palpably feelable in the physical body, as though the person is being massaged. This is the Love, with a capital 'L' to which Vimalaji referred.

Attractions or repulsions never allow you to go to the depth of love. You float on the surface; you are pulled this way or pushed that way and never arrive at love. You may know the pains of possessing and dependency, reducing persons to objects, but this is not love. Love doesn't attempt to bind, ensnare, capture. It is light, free of the burden of attachments. Love asks nothing, is fulfilled in itself. When love is there, nothing remains to be done.[2]

The 'you' cannot 'find out' what love is... Love is not an idea. It is not a thought. It is not a part of human knowledge or inheritance. It is an energy which is beyond the reach of mind or brain. It is not within the realm of causation. Hence the unconditional cessation of cerebral movement is the prerequisite of the emergence of Love. The serene silence caused by the abeyance of mental movement is the soil in which love blossoms.[3]

Once the mind is silent, and one learns the art of living in freedom from the conditioned psyche, one has affection for everything one comes across. Melting away of the ego, is arriving at love. Ego is not destroyed, it gets transformed into love. Then every movement of yours becomes an expression of love and friendship.[4]

Love which blossoms in the freedom of this illusion of time, love which blossoms in the egolessness of consciousness, has not come about because people (though they understand the illusion of this ego structure that is created) live their daily life as if the ego is a reality... As long as there is no ending of these two illusions: 1) the ego as a separate entity, necessary to be protected all the time by defence mechanisms, 2) the reality of the time-space construct – there can be neither love nor freedom in our lives today.[5]

The I-consciousness, the ego-consciousness, attached to the body and the collective conditionings disappear on the emergence of a subtler energy of Awareness, a subtler energy of Intelligence which is subtler than instinct, subtler than the intellect, much more subtle than rationality or reason. It could be called the energy of love and compassion, because love and compassion are the perfume of Intelligence.[6]

The total eradication of the narrowed-down sense of 'I-ness' and the breaking down of the walls of 'Myness' result in the sense of Wholeness of life and therefore love and compassion. And here in modern parlance when the global human conditionings and their movement end and there is a movement of the Wholeness of your being in relation to the movement of the Wholeness outside you, the movement results in what you call love and compassion.[7]

The real existential joy which is your nature, which is the nature of Intelligence, the true love and compassion... are the perfume of that ultimate Reality – joy is the attribute of that Reality. As you cannot separate liquidity from water, you cannot separate that joyfulness from the ultimate Reality, your existential nature, your existential identity.[8]

The modern civilization cannot survive unless it is inspired by ethical and spiritual values; and the most important value is love. An integrated man knows what love is and he loves everybody; a man in the relative frame of reference does not know what love is, he only knows 'lust'... The deeper dimension of man needs to be awakened through understanding with a view to express the ethical and spiritual values of love, compassion, humility, dedication and the spirit of service.[9]

DESIRE

'Desire' is a word used by Vimalaji to describe the attraction or impetus for the Brahman or Absolute to know Itself. It is also sometimes called 'Will' or 'Love' in the esoteric literature such as Theosophy, but it is not love in the human sense, rather a compelling desire or will to bring forth a dance of matter, an attraction to create or to rejoice in the dazzle of materialized Energy. The word 'desire' in the sense that Vimalaji used it, is a pure energy emanating, contained in, an attribute of the Absolute Itself, and it becomes perverted and debased when it is misinterpreted and misdirected by the human mind

which claims it and distorts it. 'Desire' is Divine Love desiring to manifest and to know Itself.

Vimalaji pointed out that there are biological needs, such as housing, clothing, food and water which should not be confused with wants. The human mind is good at transferring the need at the biological level to a want at the psychological level. Wants become all-consuming, devouring and diverting the attention from the inner quest. Wants are not even a natural part of the human life. Physical needs are indeed natural, but from these grow like weeds wishes, emotions, desires to control people, own people, own possessions, have fame and recognition, and so on. Wish is an energy, according to Vimalaji, which longs for repetition of something pleasant, and which results in attachment, addiction, infatuation, and obsession. In Vimalaji's code language, this is something quite separate from the word 'desire' which she uses to describe the 'primal energy of life.'

The primal energy of Life... is Desire. Desire is neither biologically nor psychologically stimulated. It accompanies Life wherever it is. It is an 'ingredient' of Life. In the Absolute Ground of Existence, there seems to be this primal energy of Desire which has no motivation, which has no direction, no destination....

In that emptiness of the Absolute Ground of Existence it burns bright as a flame. The word 'desire' here is not being used in the context of 'desire for something' or 'desire for someone'. Desire, as the essence of Life, is something very sacred... It does not require an effort, a human motivation for its activation.[10]

Life is limitless, it is infinite; therefore the energy of Love, the primal energy of Desire, exists without a centre, without a circumference, without a motivation, without a direction and without a destination. It is there, inexhaustible, infinite... Beyond the mind, beyond the centre of the 'me' and 'I', there is the fountain of primal energy.

Somehow religions have tried to kill this Desire, suffocate it, strangle it. And therefore you don't see any vitality or passion in the so-called religious people... there is no vitality, no freshness, no passion. What is a spiritual life if the person is not bubbling with that energy, if the person is not bubbling with love, ever fresh, ever new, ever vital? [11]

There is an energy of electricity. You want to channel it, so that you can use it for your television, refrigerator, lamps. Electricity does not exist for all these purposes. You are exploiting and gearing that energy for serving these purposes. In the same way, there is that primal energy of Desire, without which Life does not exist. The very power of movement is the result of this energy of Desire. There would be no motion in Life if there were no primal energy of Desire. The Wholeness of Life has no direction of itself, away from itself but the human race wanted to tap and exploit this energy of Desire. So they started exploiting the energy of thoughts and ideas and ideologies and sex and what have you.[12]

Thought is physical matter. Desire is a non physical energy. It has the aroma of spirituality. Thought leads to ambition and fragments life. Desire leads to aspiration and culminates into an holistic awareness of Life.

The inner, invisible world of energies is not perishable. It is a region of non-rational sensitivity. There the energy of Desire, which is a virgin energy accompanying Intelligence, has to be exercised. The stimulation of Desire provokes a sense of longing for the non-perishable state of Truth, Love and Beauty. It invokes a sense of belonging to that state of Being. The Desire and Longing for the Absolute or the Ultimate Reality changes the quality of consciousness. Instead of being interested in acquisition and possession, comparison and competition, a person gets interested in a non-acquisitive, non comparative and unconditional urge for learning.

The tragedy of the human race is contained in the mis-use of Desire. It is used to obtain objects which are not worth desiring. They are to be obtained by a conscious organised effort and they are to be used without attachment. Desire Energy is to be used for realising that which is Absolute Truth and hence desirable.

Longing for perishable objects and repetitive sensual pleasures deprives a person of his basic freedom of Being and Action. Every action of such a person covers the essence of his nature instead of uncovering it. Every movement and action builds up in his mind a false image of himself. Life is wasted in perfecting that image. An inquirer must know what is to be desired and when to use the sacred Desire Energy.[13]

If we begin to covet, to crave, to yearn for possessions, for objects, then you will weave a network of bondage around yourself... If the movement of living results in a network of bondages through the desire for acquisition, clinging, dependency, where do you find liberation or meditation? [14]

There is a difference between ambition to acquire *samadhi,* acquire transformation, obtain mutation, a difference between this acquisitive ambition centred around the ego, and a non-acquisitive urge to discover the Truth for the joy of it.

It seems to me that in human consciousness, there are these two aspirations, running parallel. There is an aspiration which is acquisitive, comparative, competitive, which wants to know, to experience, to own, to possess, on the material level, the physical level, the psychological level, etc. And there is a parallel aspiration for non-comparative, non-acquisitive, non-competitive learning, discovering, sharing, sharing of joy, sharing of peace, sharing the sorrow of one another, an aspiration to discover the goodness, the beauty. These two streams, these two currents, run parallel in human consciousness. And one has to do justice to both of them.[15]

If you want to exercise desire, use it as a bridge to commune with the Absolute, Unconditional Essence... If you go on only expanding your acquisitions and possessions on the horizontal level in relation to peripheral objects, and gratifying your repetitive needs of the body and the mind, then you do not have the privilege, the honour, the opportunity of vertically taking a quantum jump into another dimension, which is called meditation, *dhyanam, samadhi,* which is the consummation of growth.[16]

The desire for becoming liberated, for becoming transformed, blocks the way. The desire to indulge in the process of becoming does not allow the emptiness to happen. It does not allow you to become innocent, and Emptiness is innocence.[17]

When these two concepts [Brahman and Atman] are completely and totally wiped out, then the desire to attain liberation, to attain transformation, to become emancipated, will discontinue. Otherwise the desire to become emancipated or liberated becomes the greatest obstacle in the path for discovery of Truth.[18]

Note: You are still in the ego state if you want samadhi. If you are in the dimension of ISNESS, you do not want enlightenment because there is no ego and hence you cannot want it because you are already That. Once the feeling of the One Unicity, the vibration which Vimalaji calls Intelligence, is felt in the body on a more or less permanent continuum, then at this level, to want anything becomes an immediate interruption because the mind and desires intrude and ruffle the stillness. So it is almost as though we are talking about two humans, the human who thinks he or she is only a personality who needs to set a goal, and the human who has realised the reality within himself or herself, in which case, he or she needs to 'relax' as Vimalaji would say, that is, completely give oneself over to the vibration of the One Unicity, the Reality.

3. MIND AND EGO

According to Vimalaji, 'the mind is both the cause of bondage and the gate to liberation.' This is why, if we are to discover our true nature, body, emotions and mind must be controlled, but not subjugated. Working on these three aspects of human nature can be done simultaneously. Unless physical, emotional and mental desires are under control we cannot expect to achieve the mental stillness required to allow understanding of the Truth.

The human being is a construction of many layers and levels of force and energy fields. They react with each other, becoming 'fused' or integrated as the person becomes more and more aware of him or herself as many, increasingly refined energy fields. Finding great difficulty in putting this concept into words, many traditions, such as Theosophy, have attempted to describe these interpenetrating fields of energy particles as 'bodies'. Hence for example, the Alice A. Bailey books divide the mind into three 'layers' or 'bodies', for the sake of clarity, whilst simultaneously fully acknowledging the shortcomings of such symbolism.

In Vimalaji's Teaching also, based on Raja Yoga and Advaita, an equivalent explanation can be found, but using different words. There is a human inability to describe states of consciousness which are beyond our normal brain consciousness. And, because Vimalaji put great emphasis on the fact that there is one indivisible Whole, which is not divided, but differentiated, her vocabulary varied but the Teaching was the same. There is one indivisible, all-permeating Ground of Existence from which all the Energies of love and mind emerged, and into which they will again be dissolved.

*For the sake of the human brain grasping this concept, pra-
na, the astral plane, and the various 'divisions' or interpenetrating energy fields of the mind are sometimes explained
in Raja Yoga as Prakriti being 'all matter, fine and gross,
even what you call your mind, intellect and thought, because... Mind is the finest kind of matter.'* [1]

*Purusha 'has nothing to do with nature, with matter... it is
the Cosmic Self, you can call it the Seer... it is something un-
changeable, non-material, constituted of perception and understanding... so you have matter or nature on one hand including mind, and on the other you have Purusha or Self or
Atma.'* [2]

When Vimalaji discussed the self (with a small 's') as opposed
to the Self (with a capital 'S') she emphasised repeatedly that
imagining oneself to be the personality, the ego, the small 's'
self, is a mistake of incorrect perception and understanding -
avidya. The real consciousness, the Self, the Ishvara, is outside
time and space, formless and 'a mystery'. The real Self is outside
and above, a point which looks through the human eyes, 'the
Witness Thinker'.

Nature of the mind

Mind is matter, it is finest matter and what you call your
physical body is gross matter. They are really one and the
same; fine and gross, that is the only difference. Raja Yoga
says your body is the materialisation of your thought. [4]

[For the] conditioned consciousness [which] operates through
the brain the Upanishads use the term *buddhi*.. When it does
not require the operation of the cerebral organ then it is called
prajna, Intelligence... *prajna* which does not have to depend
upon any human sense organ, which is not a part of our inheritance, which is the essence of Life; and *buddhi*, the consciousness which you call the mind, consciousness functioning
through the brain. If the brain gets damaged, mutilated, then

all the knowledge that you had acquired cannot manifest
itself.[5]

There is no individual mind as far as you and me are
concerned. There is a global human mind of which there are
particular expressions in persons. The brain in you and me
has been limited. Like the narrowed-down, limited sense of
'I-ness'. Here there is the limited and bonded sense of perception. The brain feels that it knows, that it sees, but it is all
in the prison house of words, of verbalisation.[6]

We feed information, knowledge into a computer and the
computer thinks, it deduces conclusions. It has a memory, it
can respond; do you presume that the computer has an
identity or an entity? That it has an ego? You just accept it as
a mechanical movement which has been copied from the
cerebral movement of mankind. There you see very clearly
that it can happen without the 'I' consciousness, the ego consciousness. Why don't you realise that the cerebral movement taking place in this body, having the content conditioned
by humanity, has no separate point, ego or self or me? It is
something collective.[7]

No thought is my original thought. No emotion is my personal
emotion. It is the production of the collective human activity
through centuries. These feelings, thoughts and patterns of
action have been fed into my brain, like into an electronic
brain, and I respond mechanically. Although the mind is a very
beautiful, very complex and intricate instrument at our dis-
posal, it is nevertheless a machine, nothing more, nothing less
... a machine which acquires impressions through the senses.
The nervous system carries the sensation to the brain, and
the brain interprets it according to the conditioning in which it
has been brought up. Otherwise why should the word 'God'
evoke one set of feelings and thoughts in a person brought up

in a catholic family or an orthodox Hindu family, and the same word 'God' evoke quite a different feeling in a person brought up in a communist family or a communist country?... Believing in God or not believing in God is the obverse and converse of the same process.

When man sees that all mental action is a mechanistic action, then all the glory and glamour of thoughts and ideas which are organized thoughts, ideologies, conclusions and values – all the glamour and glory around this – fades away in no time. One feels no satisfaction in identifying oneself with one ideology and trying to oppose another ideology. One sees the futility of indulging in the mechanistic activity of thinking.[8]

The mental energies have a monitor called the ego, the I, the sense of Me, that assumes the role of a cohesive principle, keeping the energies of gross matter –the physical frame and the subtle matter, the mind– under its control. But the physical frame and the mental frame have an arrangement of energies which do not begin with your birth. You are the product of thousands of years of human evolution – evolution in nature and evolution in the human species. So the energies and their momentum is very ancient and the ego with the help of consciousness, finds that though it tries again and again to control the energies, the energies defy its governance. They rebel. The physical and mental frame rebels and revolts against the control, regulation, direction of the I-consciousness, the ego.[9]

Ordinarily, we live at the level where the 'I', the 'me', is the centre and the frontier is constituted by the 'not-me', by the other. Unless we divide life into the 'me' and the 'not-me', the 'I' and the 'other', the ego cannot function. It is the 'other', the 'not-me', that creates duality.[10]

The root and source of violence is in the I-consciousness and the validity of the I-consciousness is accepted by human race

as an authority. I am questioning the authority of the acceptance of this idea. Unless the human race is willing to challenge this authority, to question the authority of I-consciousness, I don't think the human race will ever be able to eliminate violence from individual or social life.[11]

The self does not really exist

The me, the self is just a concept an idea. You know in our
civilisation, the concepts are grafted on the perception. When
we look at a tree what do we see really? We see a form of
energy to which we have given a name: tree. It is a beautiful
invention of the human race to reduce a perception to a concept.

There is no 'I'. There is a body which is separate and the
body contains conditioned energy which moves and expresses
itself through perception and reaction and responses.[12]

It is only the speed, the momentum of the flow of thought that
has created an illusion of a separate 'me'... there is nothing
like an individual mind, nothing like an individual I-consciousness. Thought is the product of collective human effort
through centuries.[13]

We have to discover how [the mind] is an imagination, is an
illusion. We have to discover how this 'I', this sense of 'Me-
ness', the sense of 'My-ness', is a myth, an illusion, and how
the phenomenal world existing outside is also unreal... There
is no Vimala or Barbara inside the body. The name is given
there and by using the name frequently we feel that there is
an object inside.[14]

So what is ego then? It is wrong identification of the sense of
self-ness with the finite, with the sensory, with the psycho-

logical, just a wrong identification. That is why Vimala says, 'Ego is a psychological myth.' [15] What is ego but the crystallized images about oneself? [16]

My I-ness is composed of innumerable images that my parents had built up about me. My teachers, my friends, my relatives and myself had constructed images about myself with the help of imagination, wishful thinking, experiences, etc. The 'I' is an integrated totality of the images. [17]

The intelligence contained in our individual bodies had clothed itself into a separative I-consciousness, an ego-consciousness because of wrong identification (*asmita*). It had identified itself with the limited physical structure. It had identified itself with the mind, knowledge and the experiences of the human race. Therefore it became a separative, divisive, destructive thing. If the identification moves from body and mind, from the physical and mental to the Lord, *Ishvara pranidhanatva*, if it surrenders its existence to that supermental or transcendental essence, it no more remains the separative ego. It no more remains a destructive I-consciousness, the source of all misery. [18]

What is this 'I' ? What is this 'me'? Where does this 'I' live in my body? Where did the idea of 'me', 'mine-ness', 'I-ness', come from? When a child is born, the parents give it a name. The name is given to the body, to distinguish it from other persons. Then you call, address the child a hundred times by that name. So the first consciousness is, 'I am Harry or Robert', or whatever name I have been given. I am that. It is an identification with the name. Then the parents say: the child is very beautiful. 'I am beautiful', another identification. Then, you are Hindu, or you are a Christian, you are an Indian, you are a woman, you are a man, you are a boy, you are a girl.

So, identification goes deeper and becomes stronger with every response, and we feel that, yes, there is a 'me' inside, the 'self', the ego, and it must be preserved. How do you preserve the ego, the 'I'? You begin to give yourself everything that the 'I' demands. The 'I' says: 'I don't like that person', so we turn away. 'I like that person', then we try to possess that person, be with that person. So the preservation of the I-consciousness is really gratifying its demands, its wishes, trying to fulfil its ambitions.

I want money, I want a house, I want this, I want that, always acquisition. Acquisition of knowledge, acquisition of material goods, acquisition of experience, etc. That gives inner satisfaction, and I feel: 'Ah, yes, now I am alive.' The 'I' feels alive only in a movement: movement of acquiring or movement of reacting.[19]

Getting free from the ego

Let us not think upon thoughts and emotions and their movements as something useless. Mind is not the enemy. The conditionings are not the enemies. Our ignorance about how to use them, creates an obstacle race for us.[20]

When one has seen the futility of the movement of the 'I'... all the attachment and addiction to the 'I-ness' fades away. The 'I' with all its content is there, but it has no value for you.

In that freedom from the centre of the 'Me', you are born again. You are reborn of yourself. In the freedom from the thought structure and its movement you are born into the dimension of awareness. The sense of 'I' is then used only for the physical and biological functions. 'I am thirsty', so I drink water. You offer it to the body. The sense of 'I' is used on the biological and physical level and it has no thing, no comparison, no ambition. Do not ask how to conquer the 'I', that is the wrong way to proceed –you cannot stand on your own shoulder. See what it is, see its relevance, its futility– see it entirely and be free of its hold.[21]

The total relaxation of the mental movement is the death of the ego. There is the fear that I will be destroyed. One is not as much afraid of the physical death as one is afraid of the psychological death, the death of the ego, the discontinuity of the movement of 'I'. Because the movement of the ego has been equated with the movement of Life. And the total relaxation is being equated with death of the ego. And that fear holds you back.[22]

When the I-consciousness explodes, it gets converted into its original pristine glory of cosmic consciousness. The body along with the brain becomes a container of Supreme Intelligence, which is the expression of cosmic consciousness in the movement of relationship. This dimensional transformation is a logical consequence and a natural culmination of holistic inquiry. It is not a personal achievement. It is the privilege of anyone and everyone who has fearless readiness to live the Truth at the very moment it reveals its nature. To allow the Truth to make its abode in your consciousness and to flow freely through your neurochemical system is a great fun, accompanied by the instantaneous abolition of fear structure.[23]

4. HUMAN LIFE

I am a person who loves life tremendously. I am
passionately in love with life and nothing can divert
my attention from living. I am passionately in love
with humans and nothing can divert my attention from
friendship with humans.[1]

*Vimalaji often talks about the suitable learning conditions
which existed in the times of the Vedic period in which the
scriptures, the Vedas, were written-probably 10-15,000 years
ago. The Vedas examined all aspects of human living, and
sages, or Rishis, who had 'purified perception,' 'the ability to
communicate' and 'the strength of austerity' would teach
students who came to learn from them. The Rishis lived in
the forests and their students lived with them, absorbing
their teaching through practical living as well as through
study. This culture was shaped through collective efforts.
The Rishis were able to write the Vedas and to take students
because agricultural activity took place. The forest culture
was accompanied by agriculture, and the land was tilled
with understanding of the beauty of the soil and of growth,
rather than as happens today when agriculture descends into
a purely commercial activity.*

*In order for the individual to undergo a psychic mutation,
liberation, it was necessary for such a person to live and experience life as well as to study. In Krishi Sanskriti (agricultural culture) there was a shared reverence for the land
and its yield. It was not plundered purely for individual pro-
fit. There were kings or princes called 'rupati', pati meaning
a protector, and the responsibility of these leaders was to
protect the Rishis and the farmers.*

*Due to this integrated system, study and sadhana could flou-
rish, and wisdom could grow together with knowledge. It was
a golden age.*

*Vimalaji compares this life in which learning, cities, agri-
culture and connection with the land and animals brought
well-being and a flourishing culture of wealth –not in material possessions but wealth in happiness– with the degene-
rated state of capitalism today in which consumerism domi-
nates and the greed for possession of material objects has
become more important to human beings than a relationship
with the land, the forest, the environment and animals and
our own internal Gurudeva.*

*For this reason, in many ways communism provides a futu-
re goal –not of course a dictatorial and murderous regime
such as was imposed by Stalin– but a highly developed culture in which human beings can again be in touch with the
natural world, instead of isolated in the noise and poison of
over-crowded cities and plundered, devastated environments.
Vimalaji has pointed out that Asteya, one of the ethics for
living outlined in Patanjali's Yoga Sutras, means having :*

> a quality of consciousness which would feel it below
> its dignity to receive anything, to accept anything for
> which one has not worked... we as modern human
> beings and our societies, our governments, our ad-
> ministrations are suffering from the cancerous disea-
> se of corruption... you grab money without working
> for it, you want to have a profit much more than the
> ratio the profit allows you... I don't know if the
> Marxists or the Communists ever understood Asteya,
> but when Marx or Engel or Lenin talked about a
> society in which you take from everyone according
> to his capacity and you give to everyone according to
> his needs, without their knowing, they were refer-
> ring to the value of Asteya.[2]

*In Vimalaji's view of human culture as it should be, hu-
mans would understand their inter-connectedness with the
animals and the natural world and treat all living things
with more respect.*

Do the rivers live? Are they related with the rest of life? Earth has its own language of creativity, expressing that creativity by allowing the seeds that we sow into it to sprout and the huge trees to grow. The earth nourishes the roots of the tree with its own existential essence. Forests are the language of the earth, the communication of the earth. Trees have their own language of communication – the leaves, the fruits, the flowers, their fragrance and so on – I am trying to share with you the fact that the whole cosmos is living, interacting with every other expression of life.

Let not the human race have the vanity of imagining that it only lives and it only has relationships. The whole life is living and there are events of relationships, interactions...[3]

Therefore whatever socio-political arrangement exists within a society should allow for the freedom of the individual to relate to the natural world, to encourage the integrity of each to be able to work honestly, without taking what is not one's own in form of profits, either material or in terms of world recognition. The current system of Western capitalism does not permit such a society or culture. A system in which wealth and resources are more evenly distributed will provide for such an infrastructure, but it still depends on each individual human being to find the reason for existence and the inner Gurudeva, that form of expression of the inner flame of Ishwara. As Vimalaji explains:

The human race requires an alternative dynamics of relationship, a new base of human relationship, not memory as the base of relationship. It requires a new dimension of consciousness, a dimension of spontaneity or innocence. Physics, at the end of the 20th century, says that unless there is an awareness of the wholeness of Life, the organic wholeness of Life, the analysis of the minutest particle of matter will not reveal the nature of Life.[4]

Vimalaji strongly believed in the return of the land to the people who work the land, and for this reason as one of the leaders of the Land Gift Movement, founded by Vinoba Bhave, she mentioned that she walked 'at least 8000 miles in different parts of India, in different seasons, drenched in the heavy rains of Kerala and getting scorched on the parched up rocks and deserts in Northern India.' [4a] When Vinobaji was dying, he called her to him, and canceling all her other work, she journeyed to his bedside to bid his body farewell.

Following the Gandhian concept of village power, instead of directives and laws being imposed from above by a Central Government, Vimalaji believed that the village people should have more power in the form of local village government held by the panchayat, a local village council. Vimalaji encouraged those NGO's which fight to keep the pan-chayats free from corruption by political parties taking over what should be an independent village grass-roots government.

Vimalaji also spoke out strongly against war arguing that it was not a solution to solving problems.War was 'a psychology, it's an attitude to life, it's an approach to human problems.' [5]

For Vimalaji, the solution for prevention of war involved a new political structure, and most of all a discontinuation of corruption. The Institute of state was created as an agency to maintain law and order in society. But now the state has usurped economic, political and military power, 'and the people, whether in a welfare state or in totalitarian state or whatever, they are helpless.' [6]

For Vimalaji then, the elimination of corruption from economic, political and administrative life was an important step in the prevention of war. None of the 'isms' such as communism, Marxism, imperialism, capitalism had been successful in eradicating the roots of war, nor in providing a background in which humans could have the freedom to determine their own future through systems of the state.

For the human race to grow into the dimension of peace, Vimalaji maintained that it was necessary to attack the root

*of the problem which was the 'indecent life which we are
living today, the neurotic way of living, harbouring distrust
and mistrust of one another'.*[7]

*She explained that we have to rid ourselves of the human
conditionings which lead us to believe we are each an
individual personality, and we need to understand that there
is no separate ego, but only a universal organic wholeness.
Peace therefore will come about when political and economic
structures are reformed alongside each human being
developing an understanding of their Source, which
automatically will result in the mani-festation of the Energy
of Love.*

❖❖❖❖❖❖

Purpose of life

The purpose of life is to live; to live is to relate to the energies
within and around you without damaging them. Life itself is
Divinity. The act of living is the worship of the Divine.[8]

Patanjali says: the goal of human life is to understand the
nature of Reality, to understand the role of matter, to understand the role of energies and to understand the essence of
Intelligence. It is only understanding that liberates and ignorance that binds. We human beings feel that we are in bondage, that we are slaves of matter, that we are prisoners of
mind and thought. To us Patanjali says there is no slavery,
there is no prison house; it is only ignorance.[9]

I wonder if we are ever told that one should love life and live
it. Since childhood it is hammered into us, pursue education
for a degree, take up a job, raise a family and so on. They are
all means for living in a society. Nobody says that the purpose
of life is living and life is something sacred... To be related to
the existential essence or the Divinity of Life – that is the

main purpose of being born in a human body. So when our explorations begin, there should be the urge to learn and to educate our organism, to sensitise our organism.[10]

If life is perceived through Awareness, by dimensional shift, we can then imagine life to be like the role that one takes in a play, you try to play it perfectly, to put all the excellence of your talents into that game (but) inwardly you are aware that you are neither the hero nor the heroine, neither the prince nor the pauper.

The Cosmic Energies have their own way of functioning. There is an interrelatedness, a magnificent orderliness, a majestic harmony among all the energies, maintaining their identity without disturbing the homogeneous unity or oneness of Life, that is the Cosmic Life. If you would like to call all this as the cosmic laws or principles, you may so call them. We are related to them. We have the responsibility to live that relationship, to discharge our responsibility of contributing to that harmony, contributing to that orderliness or at least not to disturb the innate organic orderliness and harmony which seems to be the principle of Life. In human terminology, you may call it love and compassion.[11]

If the cosmos is the macrocosm, whether it is a blade of grass or a human form, then they are a microcosm, condensed cosmos, but still a cosmos. So dedication to live the truth that one understands, in the midst of society, through the movement of relationship, results in making life sacred. What more can a person hope for in one's life? [12]

Planetary consciousness

It seems to me that human beings... have been under an illusion that they are the superiors and supreme beings who are entitled to exploit all the natural resources for the gratification for their ambition and greed. The Pilgrimage towards holistic perfection, which is the essence of spirituality, will remain incomplete until this organic relationship is recognized and accepted.

Every economic or industrial development is going to prove a curse, unless the ecological and environmental sustainability is taken into consideration. All the natural resources like air, water, soil and trees are partners in human progress and participants in spiritual fulfillment. They are not dead or living objects for human consumption. The consumerist attitude towards whole life and the consumerist ambition in relation to nature are a great impediment in the transformation of human consciousness. The co-existence with nature has to be converted into a participatory comradeship, if the human species would like to equip itself for the next mutation.[13]

The Reality demands the expansion of consciousness, a sense of belonging to the whole human family, sharing the resources and the production. It is a material necessity that we develop a planetary consciousness and become conscious of our global abode, that is, the planet. If we go on plundering the planet and make it uninhabitable, then we will be heading towards racial self-extinction, extinction of the human species from the planet. The cosmos is the environment of the planet. We have to develop a sense of belonging to the whole global human family, a sense of sharing life with the whole human family, a planetary consciousness and cosmic awareness. And this cannot happen unless there is an inner psychic mutation. You may call it spiritual revolution, religious revolution, but a mutation in the very mutant, in the human consciousness, in the content of consciousness itself, is required.[14]

No sustainable society can come into existence unless [the] organic interrelation among all the innumerable expressions of life is noticed perceived, analyzed, appreciated and recognized in every human activity.[15]

No harmony can come about between the ideals of economic development, of scientific progress and the ecological and environmental sustainability, as long as economics looks upon ecology and environment as a sub-discipline, which has to be subservient to its idea of progress, prosperity and development. We in the Orient have never looked at what you call deep ecology and environment as a sub-discipline of economy. We have not looked upon economics, politics, ecology, technology, sociology as compartmentalised departments of life, having their autonomy to the extent of deciding the values cf life by themselves, so that there are separate values for economics, politics, for development and so on.

A new economic morality has to be spelt out for the world, in which human beings look upon the non-human species and non-human expressions as partners of Life, partners in production, partners in consumption of the produce. This man/nature partnership is one way towards finding a solution, if it could be called a solution. The other is looking upon the whole global human community as one family for sharing the resources of the planet.

Obviously the dynamics of human relationships and relations between the human race and nature, which has been founded upon the thesis of struggle for existence or survival of the mightiest, has to be replaced by the holistic perspective. Unity of life has to be the foundation for socio-economic, political structures.[16]

MAN AND SOCIETY

The science of yoga helps us to learn how to balance the biological energies, how to purify them, how to harmonise them. This is part of self-education. No individual can contribute to the social welfare, to the ascendance of society, the

cultural growth or prosperity of society unless within himself
or herself the person arrives at this state of equanimity, equipoise, equibalance.[17]

[Meditation] is the foundation for social action. Today social
action is taken up by people whose minds are not balanced...
So social action is motivated somewhere by personal ambition
and that social action cannot bring about any basic transformation in socio-economic structures. We want now a transformation that will take place on two fronts simultaneously: 1)
in individual consciousness and 2) in social structures.[18]

The meditative way of life transforms the individuals into...
human beings who have love and care, tenderness and affection for one another. Then only we can hope for a human
society based on freedom and equality; and it is the only hope
for the world.[19]

If I talk about the dynamic force of love, people just don't believe. If you talk about a revolution brought about through the
dynamism of love and co-operation, they say no, it cannot be.
You have to teach people to hate. You have to provoke their
jealousy and hatred against one another. Hatred and anger,
jealousy and violence have been used as motivation forces for
revolutions, and now is the challenge to replace them by the
dynamic force of love and cooperation. Then we will bring
about socio-economic, political, cultural, international changes,
in a decent, human way.[20]

The root and source of violence is in the I-consciousness and
the validity of the I-consciousness is accepted by the human
race as an authority. I am questioning the authority of the
acceptance of this idea. Unless the human race is willing to
challenge this authority, to question the authority of I-cons-

ciousness, I don't think the human race will ever be able to eliminate violence from individual or social life.[21]

Total revolution

The challenge is a total revolution which will work in the individual and the collective simultaneously, which will work in the inside as well as the outside simultaneously, and the revolution will take place exactly where we are, in the midst of people, in the midst of human relationship. That is why I call it a total revolution, not a partial, not a fragmentary one. We have not got any precedent in history for such a total revolution.[22] ... a revolution in the inner quality of consciousness which will be reflected into and extended to the social, economic and political relationships. It's no use trying to bring about changes in fragments or factions of life. Such fragmentary revolts may affect the momentum of a total revolution instead of accelerating its speed.[23]

Revolutions will have to be total and the beginning will have to be made in individual life. Initiative will have to be taken by the individual who will be a living centre of a new revolution. But he will be a centre of revolution only when he does not run away from his daily life in the name of religion and spirituality, when he faces the challenge of transforming the quality of his behaviour.[24]

The challenge in the developing countries in Asia is of finding out a way of total revolution. Changing the outer, but simultaneously changing the inner too. We have to realize that the roots of all aggression, exploitation, injustice, violence, are in our heart. The roots are in the individual psyche.[25]

A social activist who spends regularly some time in prayer and meditation realises that he is not a social worker, doing work for other people, but he is a *sadhaka*, a *jivan sadhaka*, who does everything for his own benefit, for his own upliftment, his own purification. It is only a *jivan sadhaka* who can become a Sarvodaya revolutionary. In other revolutionary movements, workers are educated and trained to work out certain methodologies, strategies, ideologies; but in Sarvodaya one has to begin to work just for the transformation, for the revolution, first in one's own life.

Sarvodaya begins with an inner revolution, an inner transformation in the individual; and then it spreads over to society... We do the work because it is our need, not to oblige others, not with the expectation that we will get something back in return. We do it because we cannot live otherwise. It is an inner compulsion of love, of compassion and understanding of truth, love and non-violence; that becomes the religion of the revolutionary, the Sarvodaya revolutionary.[26]

A new type of society

Work is an expression of love, but where? Not in a competitive society. The human being has developed a social, economic and political structure where he finds himself a misfit. Because the human animal is not fitted to live in monstrously huge cities, to work in monstrously huge units of production where there is no personal relationships. He does not deserve to live in a society where the producer and the consumer have no direct relationship, in a depersonalised, dehumanised surrounding.

So a religious inquirer who is deeply concerned with the discovery of reality, totality, meditation, freedom, very soon finds himself incapable of going back to society. And I would say: 'Why go back, then?' I think in agriculture, in gardening, in the villages, in small communities, it must be possible to experiment with an alternative way of living where one does not have to enter the competitive and the comparative life.[27]

A person who is anxious to see that there is peace in the world will never cooperate with the efforts of society to project and stimulate wars. If he is punished by that society, he will go through that punishment –that is part of the game. If he cannot find a job and has to suffer and starve, the starvation will be regarded as part of the game. But he will in no case compromise with this society and take up a job which will in any way, directly or indirectly, contribute to the stimulation, provocation, or actual operation of war... He will not cooperate with exploitation, with efforts to create war, with efforts to isolate or divide humanity in the name of race, religion and country.[28]

A genuine democracy free from the clutches of consumerist capitalism and autocratic totalitarianism, is a long way to go. Parliamentary representative democracy is still an utopia. Government of the people, by the people and for the people, is only an idea. Political parties with their vested interests have appropriated the state through criminalized politics. Organised and institutionalised religions have corrupted the human psyche through sanctioning beliefs, superstitions, traditions and ritualism... It's a long way to awaken peace and harmony in individual or collective life.

The individual is psychologically structured and intellectually programmed to demand lucrative jobs and fit himself as a cog into the dehumanized and depersonalized global economic structure... Ruthless assertiveness and aggressive competition along with harsh commercialization of life are supreme values of modern life.

The mono superpower, USA, wants to monitor and direct world affairs in order to retain its nuclear supremacy... It wants to conceal from its own people the grim reality of the economic recession, stagflation, loss of prestige in the world... [and] cultural decay. With the disintegration of the USA will dawn an era of a new world order... preceded by economic chaos and political anarchy.

The emerging compulsions will pressurize the human psyche to investigate, explore and experiment a world order based on sharing the planetary resources equitably. Cosmic awareness, planetary consciousness and global sharing might perhaps become the fundamental principles of the 21st century.[29]

'The world needs today a United Peoples' Organisation, not the United Nations Organisation. We need a United Peoples' Organisation where the representatives of the people will come together to share their problems, to find out how to share the resources of the earth.[30]

The architects of tomorrow should meet together and explore the possibility of establishing 'Education for Survival Centres' in as many countries as possible. It might require a global human fraternity, with global activists willing to work at the location where they are living.

Such an educational centre should be called 'Global Educational Centre for Human Survival' It should not seek patronage or financial help of the governments of the State or any political parties of the country. Patronage should be sought from International or Global Institutions and organisations who are non-political in nature and humanitarian in character, e.g., UN, SAARC, Amnesty International, World Goodwill, etc.

Such an educational centre would endeavour to educate the members in:

- Ecological and environmental consciousness,
- Planetary peace and prosperity projects,
- Exploration in alternative energies,
- Alternative technology,
- Wholistic healing,
- Dimensions of holistic peace.[31]

India

Vimalaji had once written that Indian civilization had only one aim which was to ensure that human beings should arrive at the consummation of their holistic growth in the state of Yoga, which was, she explained, equanimity inside, and balance at the sensual level.

The Land Gift Movement of which Vimalaji was one of the leaders, was a part of the great saga, the great journey of India, in which the hidden light had to be protected from being crushed and extinguished. The Land Gift Movement was a part of the great wave of social revolution that swept India during the fight for independence, and following. It was instrumental in preventing an uprising of the proletariat, in its place encouraging a democratic and voluntary redistribution of land from the rich landowners to the landless villagers.

The word 'secular democracy' has played havoc in the Indian consciousness. The word has been borrowed from Europe, where the Church and the State used to be in cons-tant conflict and tension. Therefore it was necessary to de-clare that the State and its Government would be entirely secular. In other words, the authority of organised religion would not deprive the State of its sovereignty.

The dimension of Adhyatma, i.e., spirituality, was not known to the West. Atma Vidya or the science of consciousness was the discovery of the Asian Sages and Seers. If the words 'spiritual democracy' were used in the Constitution, the unwarranted chaos and political stagnation which we see around ourselves would have been avoided.

It is true that the Indian people are religious-minded but this is only half the truth. The Hindus, the Muslims, the Buddhists, the Jains, the Sikhs and the Christians are spontaneously aware of the infinity and eternity of Life. They are aware that there is only one Divinity that is worshipped in different ways by different communities.[32]

The transmission of the Indian Cultural Heritage which implies the recognition of wholeness and homogeneity of Life has been arrested since perhaps Indian Independence. The onslaught of materialistic consumerist culture of the West has resulted in a pathetic collapse of the Indian way of living and the Indian perspective of life. Hence the revival of the Vedic Culture is urgently needed. Faith in the Supreme Cosmic intelligence, trust in Man, reverence for life and friendliness towards all is the essence of Vedic Culture. Its revival shall wash off all the pettiness, cowardice and diffidence which has polluted the Indian psyche.[33]

5. SPIRITUALITY - YOGA

Sprituality is freedom from the centre of the me.[1]

*If Brahman, the Divinity is the infinite, all-permeating Es-
sence which is indivisible and which interpenetrates all matter, then the question arises as to why a person needs to seek
the Godhead. Vimalaji's answer to this is that human beings
are obsessed with the sense of duality. We live 'in the conditioned physical organism operating through the conditioned
consciousness, where the act of relating to life is based upon
the imaginary division as subject and object'. On the contrary, there is another means of perceiving the world from, or
emerged within, a dimension which is free of time, space
and consciousness, for the three are intimately connected. If
life is perceived through Awareness, as a result of a dimensional shift taking place in us, we can then 'imagine life to be
like the role that one takes in a play, you try to play it
perfectly, to put all the excellence of your talents into that
game (but) inwardly you are aware that you are neither the
hero nor the heroine, neither the prince nor the pauper'.
Aware of your own ISNESS, perfected completion, you still
play the role.*

*Vimalaji said that 'If you are aware that the duality gene-
rated by the limited sense organs and the conditioned psychology are not the ultimate reality, if you are aware that the
indwelling Essence – the indwelling Reality in every expression of life– is the same, then you become aware of the unity
of life; you become aware of the foundation of non-duality on
which the game of duality is played'. In other words, the inquiry, the sadhana, is necessary in order to understand that
there is no dualism. It is not enough to merely have knowledge that the underlying Absolute all-permeating Energy is a
Unicity, it has to be realised first through effort and then
later through non-effort.*

Spirituality means the quietening down, the cessation of our thinking, our conditioned stream of thought. Behind the physical and emotional kind of energy which we function in daily life, lies a dimension of a totally different quality from which we must learn to function... Spirituality as a way of life teaches us to get into contact with the inner silence in ourselves. Only thereby is it possible to be aware of that totally different source. This religious way of life is based on the ancient Indian yoga teachings. When one starts searching for all kinds of experiences, one places oneself in the centre and actually does nothing else but extends one's horizontal level, while with spirituality the point is getting into contact with the vertical dimension. We should start functioning from there. I'm not saying that increasing ones knowledge or gathering experiences are to be condemned. This however is not spirituality.[2]

Spirituality is a science of life: they call it physics of consciousness. As physics tries to explore the nature of Reality through analyzing matter and energy, spirituality explores the nature of Ultimate Reality by analyzing the nature of consciousness. Let us be very clear that spirituality is a science of life, it is not related to any beliefs, traditions or dogmas.[3]

Spirituality has nothing to do with the concept of God whatsoever. We have created a conceptual structure as a psychological necessity and in the conceptual structure all religions have indulged in this concept of God or Godhood. But spirituality does not begin with the assumption that there is a God —personal or impersonal— that created the universe. ... In the Veda someone asks the Sage:

Question : *Who created this universe ?*
Answer : There is no creator apart from the creation.
Q : *What was the cause of creation ?*
A : It is a causeless cause, it is its own cause, it is its own effect.

Q : *But there must be some creator to the universe ?*
A : Where is the universe ? The universe is within you, in your mind.[4]

As you in the West have seen this whole panorama of scientific investigation into the external world, so the Orient has seen the panorama of an inner investigation. Spirituality is a science of Life. It has nothing to do with credulity, beliefs, the world of make-believe or wishful thinking or any such emotional stuff and nonsense that goes by the name of spirituality. It is a science as precise as the science you know in the West. But here the exploration and investigation have taken place within, not without. Secondly, it has taken place without the help of any instruments whatsoever. It has been a non sensual and non-psychological, non-cerebral exploration, experimentation of the space within.

Those who have never heard about it or have not seen such experiments, such explorations taking place, find it hard to believe. They find it difficult to believe, for example, that the emptiness of space is full of creative energies, difficult to understand that silence and relaxation can release energy.

Mental movement is irrelevant to the investigation and exploration of Reality. Mind moves through time. Mind moves with the help of concepts. Mind cannot leave words or verbalisation behind. So one may say: 'If I cannot further explore through the mind, let me experiment with total relaxation of the mind.' We have moved from the world of argumentation, logic, speculation to the world of investigation through personal experimentation. Speculation and games of logic have no scope in this area. This is what hurts the ego of mankind. It cannot come about by reading books about spirituality. One is not talking about new rituals, but experimentations which require dedication to the cause and determination to devote some time and energy.[5]

Spirituality implies functioning, operating and acting in daily life. If one turns one's back to the world, one accepts one's relations with the world to become severed. But experience of the divine can only manifest in the here and now. In relating to each other and to the world, there is life, there is freedom. Escape from daily reality prolongs the sense of alienation and schizophrenia. Consciousness is: being-in-relation-with. Again, there is no other life than life in relationship because the root of it is the Oneness of which all of us are parts.[5]

Renunciation is the austerity to welcome that which life brings to my door steps, not to reject what life brings and not to seek what is not brought to me; the austerity to walk through the pain and pleasure of life, the corridors of insults and flatteries, without getting stuck up anywhere.[6]

Discovery of what Truth is, of what God is, of what the Reality of life is, is not full of security. Everything is not very smooth there. There are no blueprints. To let the total mental activity cease to function, to let the ego into abeyance and to be with the unknown is not a game of security. It needs a kind of fearlessness to come face to face with that which is not mapped out. An inquirer going within and taking a voyage into himself makes his own path.[7]

The question may arise: 'What will happen? What shall I get?' The 'I' shall not get anything at all. If the 'I' withdraws to silence with the hope, the expectation, the ambition of developing some extraordinary powers or having some occult experience, then it carries the tension of that expectation, hope or ambition. The 'I' shall not get anything. The 'I' that has created an enclosure which may be necessary on the physical and psychological level, comes out of it voluntarily, and relaxes. I have nothing to see, nothing to obtain, nothing to acquire, nothing to experience, just be with myself. We are never quite with ourselves, are we? We are always the father, the mother, the husband, the wife, the businessman. We are always functioning like machines, carrying out one role or another.[8]

HUMAN EVOLUTION

The Pilgrimage [towards Divinity] begins with the recognition of the animality. The human species must recognise that they carry in their physical organism tremendous inheritance of animality. The human form is the product of biological, cosmic evolution through untold centuries. There has been progressive refinement and re-organisation in the autonomous systems functioning within the form. It is rightly said that a human being is a rational animal. The animality has to be accepted, identified and respected. Autonomous instincts such as appetite, thirst, sleep and urge for procreation are common to all the human and non-human species.

The momentum of the biological instincts is irresistible. The instincts get activated in a rhythmic way and they cannot be ignored, denied or repressed. To adjust the rhythm and the cycle of the instinctive activation with the human requirement of social life is to begin a cultural pilgrimage towards perfection. The rational and scientific adjustment with the biological instincts is to respect the phenomenon of human coexistence with nature.

The second phase of Pilgrimage begins with the recognition of gigantic racial inheritance that we carry in the neurochemical system of the body. The human beings are the product of human civilisation and culture through millions of centuries. 'Culture' implies organisation and harmony. The human brain has been trained in the art of organising the amalgamated knowledge, experience and patterns of psychophysical behaviours in such a harmonious way that one can operate smoothly as a member of society. The human inheritance activates electronic impulses which we call thoughts, feelings, sentiments, etc. The momentum of these organic impulses yields to control. But it cannot be eliminated completely.

Now begins the third phase of human Pilgrimage towards Divinity with the use of self-conscious energy, with which the human species has emerged out of the animal kingdom. The human race has awakened to the awareness of trans-mental dimension. It has awakened into the science of non physical energies, that is spirituality. The human race has moved from theology to spirituality from rationality to spontaneity and entered into a partnership with cosmic energies. The individual has taken a vertical quantum jump from neurochemical to the dimension of Silence, full of vibrating ethereal energy. The transcendence from the total biological and psychological energies transforms the isolated individual into a living expression of the wholeness of Life. The physical form remains a relatively independent entity, but the brain and mind get converted into sacred instruments of expression in charge of the Supreme ISNESS of cosmic life, which we call Divinity.

The humanness and the Divineness meet at the altar of meditation. The transfusion of both creates a mutated being who is called a yogi. Yogis are a race by themselves, though their physical form resembles that of unmutated common human animals. The yogis live in the dimension of *samadhi* which is a holistic awareness of the totality of Life, whereas the common human being is governed by individualistic self-consciousness.[9]

Divinity is nothing but refined humanity. If a human being goes on refining himself, at all the layers of his being, the essence of Divinity, which is unconditional love, compassion, intelligence, spontaneous understanding, etc., will begin to manifest through that human being. Divinity has to express itself through some form and that person gets converted into the vehicle for the Supreme to manifest, to express. That is what a yogi is. [10]

To allow the Divinity or the Absolute Truth to use your body, your brain, your mind for the service of humanity is one thing. 'I want to serve and I get pleasure out of that service. I'm serving so and so, the cause or the individual' There is pleasure in that. But to let go of that pleasure and allow the Truth to shape your life, to mould it, to give it a direction and to use it for the cosmic purpose, requires tremendous fearlessness. And very few are willing to let go of the last noble pleasure for that.[11]

A human being born of the cosmic energy is susceptible to the rulings of that Intelligence. A person in a truly egoless state is thereby a tool for the cosmic Intelligence to serve cosmic purposes.[12]

A radical mutation in the quality of human consciousness will take place. We are concerned with preparing the ground for the emergence of a new human race.[13] By offering our life for that psychological mutation we might be creating a new cell, a new life style, a new way of living, by which we might be setting into the human orbit of consciousness a spark of love and compassion. So let us not forget that we are embarking upon the adventure of religious enquiry, not for petty little self-centred activity or cultivating 'kundalini power', *shaktipat* or astral and occult experiences. But we embark upon that enquiry on behalf of the whole human race.[14]

Question: Do you believe in a life hereafter?
Vimalaji: I do not understand the term 'hereafter'. The physical body dies or disintegrates. Thought being a conditioned energy does not die, cannot be destroyed. It continues. It was there before the physical form got shaped and shall continue to vibrate. Hence thought is ever alive.

Question: Do you subscribe to the theory of Rebirth and Law of Karma ?

Vimalaji: The Law of Karma is a law that governs the material, biological world. Reap as you sow... in human life there is a psycho-physical dimension replacing the barely biological one. The law of karma governs the psychological as well as the biological level among the human beings. It is a psycho-somatic realm where the law of karma is still applicable and is valid.

As thought does not die, the term Rebirth applies to the re-emergence of Thought when it gets clothed in a new human form. Thought is reborn. If thought is transcended, no vibrational residue is left behind at the event of death. Persons living in the dimension of *samadhi* terminate irrevocably at the moment of death. There is no relevance of Rebirth or continuity to such beings. [15]

SADHANA

A person who is interested in finding out what is beyond the mind and thought, what is beyond the world of concepts and symbols, will have to learn to be in a state of non action. Nobody has been educated on those lines, so we begin self-education or *sadhana* as they call it in India. [It is said in] the Upanishads that it is not for gaining something which you have not, because there is nothing in the cosmos that the individual does not possess within himself.

Then why is *sadhana* necessary? To remove the obstacles in the path of realizing one's own nature. We have surrounded ourselves with so many things, physically, psychologically, with so much knowledge. It is not very encouraging for the people when they come to learn that through *sadhana* there is nothing to be acquired; everything is to be understood as it is,

and to enable ourselves to live in the light of that understanding which we carry in ourselves.[16]

The intelligence contained in our individual bodies had clothed
itself into a separative I-consciousness, an ego-consciousness
because of wrong identification *asmita – vipirit asmita.* It had
identified itself with the limited physical structure. It had
identified itself with the mind, the knowledge and the experiences of the human race. Therefore it became a separative, divisive destructive thing. If the identification moves from
body and mind, from the physical and mental to the Lord,
Ishvara pranidhanatwa, if it surrenders its existence to that
supramental or transcendental essence, it no more remains the
separative ego. It no more remains a destructive I-consciousness, the source of all misery.

Purification will come through two processes. One is allowing
all the mental movements to go into abeyance – which is
Silence. It leads you to meditation. And another is to educate
the system, to set itself free from *avidya, asmita, raja, dwe-
sha, abhinevesha.* Correct the identification – that is all. It is
the nature of *chitta* to remain identified somewhere. If it remains identified with the physical body, it will succumb to the
bodily impulses, drives, pushes and pulls. If it identified with
mind, knowledge, experience, it will succumb to, it will be
overwhelmed by the whole human past. Hence the identification has to be corrected.

Who is going to correct the identification? Through the individualisation, distribution of energies into different organs,
through the diversification of their functions, we were separate from the *mula prakriti* or the universal matter. In this
hour of relaxation, in this hour of surrender, the separation
comes to an end. This is called *samadhi. Samadhi* is the cave
in which the revelation will take place. It is only now a
question between *mula prakriti* and *Brahman.* It is only a
question between *maya* and *Ishvara.* You have already crossed from *jiva* to *mula prakriti* or *maya.*[17]

When you see... [that] life is a cycle of emergence and merging back, emergence and dissolution – then you do not pay undue importance to birth and death, then you do not pay undue importance to what happens through you, claiming it to be yours, not getting despondent because something goes wrong with you, through you. You follow the upward path of refinement, purification, harmonization of energies and the rest follows.[18]

The act of living is the field of *sadhana*. Your homes are the centres. They can become the ashrams for *sadhana*. Every relationship becomes an opportunity to discover the factual content of our mind and then correct it. So relationships become the opportunities for self discovery.[19]

Those who isolate themselves from the mainstream of day-to-day life by going to some monastery or ashram, retiring from the responsibilities of day-to-day life, to transform the quality of their inner life, indulge in a fragmentary action. The time is now ripe to have an integrated approach in which there will be equal emphasis on both, the inward and outward trans-formation.[20]

You see the Rishis of the *Upanishads* never talk about re-nunciation; they only talk of restraint – the capacity of self-restraint. And they think the capacity of self-restraint is the essence of human culture. The capacity of self-restraint is the secret of harmony. They are lovers of Life and the *Upani-shads* are the songs of love, they are burst of joy in the event of communion with life... spontaneous equanimity of the sensual level and elegant tranquillity on the psychological level; they together constitute the essence of Yoga, the essence of meditation, the essence of enlightenment or liberation.[21]

The word *brahmacharya* has been narrowed down to mean celibacy, continence, refraining from sex life... Celibacy is a very limited thing. Married life or sexual relationship, if it is not distorted, if it is a normal, healthy part of human life... is not an obstacle... to the dedication, to the Truth of Life.[22]

The sex energy is the expression of creativity that we share with the Divinity. When that energy is exercised with a self-restraint, a healthy and sane self-restraint, then that energy is not only retained locally, it permeates the whole being. Then that vital energy – the essential creativity, the existential essence of our being – is communicated through the eyes, through the speech and through the sex. If there is an education in a sense of restraint and aesthetically responsible exercise of these energies, then those energies going back to their source of silence and emptiness, permeate the whole being, permeate every drop of the blood. The person becomes vital, sharp and alert like the blade of a sword. The organic, perceptive sensitivity which may be the essence of Divinity, Chaitanya, Atman, that becomes operative through every drop of the blood, every word of the mouth and every glance of the sight.[23]

One needs to have at least twelve hours per day alone –this means if you sleep eight hours per night you would have four hours alone. You have seen how Vimala goes into a room and shuts the door, and does not open it for anybody or anything. As one needs to wash the body every day to keep it clean, so also one needs to wash the psyche in Silence every day to keep it pure. This practice is especially necessary when one is leading a busy life of social action. A person who is exploring the dimension of meditation, exploring the dimension of non-motion, silence, emptiness, will have to turn to the other aspect of daily life. You will have to create a supportive way of living, a way of living that is supportive to the establishment of inner silence. What will we do to create a supportive way of living? We will minimise verbalisation as far as possible. This is the way we will have to educate ourselves.[24]

If you can communicate in one sentence, then you will not use ten sentences for that. Because every verbalisation is the emanation of sound energy from your body which carries with it the fire energy also. It is an emanation of prana, the fire principle, and also nada, the sound principle. With excessive verbalisation, that vital energy is spent and consumed recklessly... As an educator of myself, as a *sadhaka,* as a self enquirer, I will minimise the outgoing activity... The outgoing energies are restricted but they are not suppressed. Every individual will educate himself or herself in his or her own unique way. It is said, 'There are as many paths of self-inquiry as there are individuals.' Minimum guidelines can be provided, but the actual *sadhana* has to be conducted with utter freedom, unconditional freedom, uninhibited freedom. Unless you conduct it out of your freedom, there will be no sense of responsibility. You will throw the responsibility on the teacher, the master, the Guru, and you will lapse into the sluggishness of insensitivity. You may lapse back into psychological inertia and mistake it for humility.

The inner and the outer have to be harmonised. You cannot be licentious in physical living, disorderly in mental living, imbalanced in psychological behaviour, and then inquire about meditation, transformation and mutation.[25]

What is the obstacle on the path of a *sadhaka?* This nothingness and nobodyness [of the state of silence]. To go through that period of silence is difficult, especially for those who are living in big cities; they have a job, they have families. Unless they move away from their working place and family atmosphere for some time, this education from the doer, the experiencer to the Seer, from the Seer into the Silence and then into meditation, this education cannot happen.[26]

GURU AND DISCIPLE

Vimalaji once likened a group of yoga students from Eu-rope to the Forest Universities held in the Vedic period when students sat at the feet of Sages and learnt from the example the Teacher had to offer, from life experience and additionally from esoteric spiritual knowledge, transmitted by the Teacher.

'We shall go back as we had done last year', she said to them at the beginning of her first talk, 'to the ancient forest University of the Upanishads, to learn from the Sages of ancient India. The Sages, who taught in a very poetic way, who were concerned with living a life full of bliss, love and relaxation, whose primary concern was to discover the meaning of Life, the mystery of Creation, the nature of Ultimate Reality and our relationship with that Reality.'

'The disciple, *she said,* needs to have the capacity for listening, receiving, containing, and living the teaching. Otherwise whatever the teacher says will be heard and thrown or dumped into memory. It does not affect the quality of consciousness and therefore has no bearing upon the texture of human relationship.'[27]

Vimalaji in these talks[28] explained that

The [Teacher] was called a *Rishi* because the word *Rishi* is derived from the Sanskrit root which implied 'to perceive'. *Rishi* is an individual whose perceptions are purified. In English you call them a sage, but the word 'sage' does not explain the nuances contained in the word *Rishi. Rishi* means purified perception, austerity to live the perception as it has taken place, and the capacity to teach if students come to them. *Rishis* must have these three:

> 1. Purified perception: they can perceive the sound and the quality of sound, they can perceive light and the constituent principles of light and they can per-

ceive even where perceptions are subtle, fine, purified.

2. The strength of austerity – rather, the strength to
dedicate one's life to living of Truth. You can perceive the truth but you may not live it. Then you
cannot be called a *Rishi*. ...

3. The capacity to communicate. If the student came
to learn, then you can take the role of a teacher and
communicate.

*Vimalaji explained that an 'inquirer reaches home, the land
of liberation, by consulting, by discussion with the people
who have known the land of liberation, who have been to the
land of liberation and enjoyed the bliss of freedom'* [29] *but it
is difficult to find any passage in any talks or books where
she herself claimed to be a Teacher. And perhaps this great
humility was born of the understanding that every person is
equal in their divinity, but simply that some have yet to
understand the content of that Divinity within their own
being.*

*Vimalaji had written to one of her friends that 'there are no
supports and crutches in the dimension of Silence... I do not
allow anyone to develop a personal relationship with me.'*

One day I grew bolder. 'I know Vimalaji does not like the word
"disciple", I said, but I feel that I am Vimalaji's disciple in the
Vedic sense of the term, in the sense that Vimalaji has caused
the awakening of the awareness in a hastened process due to
her interaction with Christine.'

How could I have said it! She had constantly refused to accept
the word (not the fact) of discipleship, because it led to a sense
of dependency and worship. She knew that, an important pre-
condition of liberation was total freedom from all dogma, from
all concepts, from all claims of special rela-tionships. But with
great love and compassion which seemed to stream from her

being, Vimalaji answered that Christine could use the word 'Teacher' and the word 'disciple'.

— (Christine Towend, *The Hidden Master*, Motilal Banarsidass, 2002)

A disciple is one who is ever receptive and ever learning. As per my perception, the word *sishya* has no other content. A Master, a Guru, is one who has fathomed the source of Reality and lives in daily life from that fountain of Energy. It is the living of Truth which entitles a person to be called a Guru or a Master.

'I-amness' is the primary light... and 'Guru' means that person from whose consciousness the darkness of ignorance has receded completely. Guru is one who lives in the light of that primal energy, who lives at the source of the cosmos.[30]

And who can be called a teacher? The [*Ishavasya*] Upanishad has given us the word *kavi;* one who penetrates the manifest, who sees the unmanifest and even that which is unmanifestable, who sees the visible, penetrates the invisible and is capable of feeling the infinite is a *kavi*. What else constitutes the teacher? *Manishi,* another word that was given to us. The perception of reality has penetrated his who-le mind, the perception of the limitless, the unnameable, the immeasurable, the indescribable, the awareness of that, the perception of that, has penetrated the limited, the conditioned, the mind, the thought structure.

... a Guru, a teacher is not supposed to talk out of knowledge though he may have tremendous knowledge. One who talks out of knowledge or deep study can be called a philosopher, he can be a scholar, he can be a pundit, but the vastness and deepness of knowledge which is verbal knowledge, which is only indirect perception, does not enable you to be a teacher, a master, a guru.

The Teacher has the indirect perception of Reality through knowledge and the direct communion with Reality through the activation of Intelligence, and that communion with Reality, that activation of intelligence, that direct perception, that direct contact and personal encounter is manifested in the behaviour, in the relationship with others. If this does not happen he is not a teacher. One who talks about Reality is not a teacher, one who writes about it, one who sings hymns to it, one who can compose poetry about it, one who can paint pictures or create pieces of sculpture is not a teacher unless he lives in communion with Reality and it is manifested in his behaviour.

How does the teacher reveal the Divinity or Reality in his life? The being, the presence of the teacher has a steadiness and firmness; the being is rooted in peace, in steadiness. The physical presence has a peace, there is no unsteadiness about the physical being, there is a feeling of reliability, of stability... The teacher cannot help the student to dispel the darkness of ignorance, if the words are not precise, if the glance of the teacher is not precise, if it is wavering, if it is flickering, then the student cannot be helped. Truth does not flicker... there is reliability in the presence and reliability in the speech.

A teacher is not a person whose physical behaviour would be imbalanced, confused, chaotic, because the Intelligence that was awakened percolates right down to the senses... The Intelligence is revealed, the order of the Cosmos is revealed in the manifest, in the world of forms, and therefore the Teacher is a person in whom the Supreme Intelligence, the clarity, the holiness, the tenderness of love is manifested, is reflected, is expressed in the being and in the behaviour.[31]

An enlightened one, a liberated one, is a person in whom this repetitive, mechanistic, conditioned movement [of the brain] has discontinued and an unconditioned energy perceives. So it is a perception including understanding – not two things like seeing and then having knowledge. Perception is understanding and so enlightenment. Here is 'perception', there 'liberation' from the sense of Iness. Here it is liberation from the

conditioned global mental movement and global human conditionings. It is only different ways of looking at the same
thing...[32]

If an enquirer needs help then life sees to it that the enquirer
and the one whose understanding has blossomed are brought
together. Teacher and disciple will meet. Disciple means one
who is willing to learn. Master is a person whose enquiry has
blossomed into understanding. So such a meeting is brought
about by life... [by] the grace of God or whatever you call it.
I think the universal intelligence is eager to help when we are
charged with the enquiry, when the intensity of learning is
there. Then such a meeting takes place. Something gets transmitted between the two and it is over. You cannot create a
psychological relationship and say, this is my master or this is
my disciple. How can you have a psychological relationship
with one who has no centre, no ego? He lives in consciousness without a centre. The unlit candle got lit and both have
independent lives. Love, respect and gratefulness is there, but
you cannot say, 'my master'. Our minds are not prepared to
see such facts. So we convert the happening to possession,
ownership. We create a psychological relationship.[33]

When a person transcends the frontiers of the conditioned
brain, when a person has grown into an entirely new dimension of consciousness, which has no centre and no periphery
at all, with whom are you going to have a static relationship
and say, 'This is my master and I am his pupil' ? Beyond the
frontiers of mind there is no time and space... the person is
living in the dynamic motion of love and awareness. How are
you going to arrest the movement of that person's life and
bind him in a static relationship, to claim: 'Here is my guru,
here is my master'? You cannot capture the breeze that
comes to you in your fist and say, 'this is my breeze'! How
are you going to impose psychological relationship on a person

who has become nothingness, because there is no ego, there is no I-consciousness? It is the universal consciousness blowing through that individual and singing the song through that flesh and those bones. The individual is no more there.[34]

The outer master functions as a bridge, as it were, because there is a gap created by the thought structure between the intelligence and the senses and sense organs. And the master says: '... see what I do, listen to what I say, observe how I live, and get to the real guru, the inner guru, the Atman, the Intelligence, Life, the master par excellence, the supreme master.' [35]

The word Guru cannot be imposed permanently upon a person. It indicates a state of consciousness. And the word disciple (*sishya* ou *chela)* also indicates a state of inquiry, receptivity. And receptivity attracts love and freedom as the scorched earth after the summer season attracts the rains and get new life when the clouds descend and bathe it with the waters of life. An enquirer can never been lonely. He does not have to worry about who is going to guide him or instruct him. Leave that to Life. Leave that to the law of love. Be concerned with the honesty, the integrity and the intensity of your own inquiry, correlate it with all the life and leave the rest to Life itself.[36]

Vimalaji as teacher

The relationship between the teacher and the student is something sacred. I am involved as far as correcting their imbalances are concerned. I am not involved if they cry. I just ignore their tears. If their ego is hurt, I just ignore it. I am involved to the extent that the purpose for which they come is not forgotten by them. It's a beautiful way of living.[37]

As long as the person [i.e., guru] is alive there is a great significance in the interaction of energies with such a person. In this part of the globe that is called 'satsang' living around, living with a person who has committed himself or herself to the perception, the discovery of the Truth, by embodying the Truth discovered in every breath, every word, every deed. So such Gatherings have not only relevance but great psychic vitality. But when [the guru] departs, then keeping the photograph, placing the videos or audio cassettes, can generate a sect, can build an enclosure and transmit the enclosure to the other enquirers. Let us save ourselves from such an irresponsible action Let us protect ourselves from the eventuality.

[It is] our responsibility – yours and mine – to see that we conduct ourselves in such a way that after our departure no traces are left behind which could generate a sect, an artificial enclosure in the psyche of the human being. It would be a crime on my part to allow the celebration [of Vimala's birthday] to continue and a sense of responsibility obliges me to restrain the emotions and sentiments of my friends who love and respect me.[38]

There are no supports and crutches in the dimension of Silence... I do not allow anyone to develop a personal relationship of a Master-Disciple with me. I am a teacher who teaches in an impersonal way, even in personal dialogues or in group meetings.' [39]

Without false modesty Vimalaji can claim that the source of Ultimate Reality is no more a theory or an abstraction for her. She lives in the Divinity that has been fathomed, but Vimala has not initiated anyone according to the Indian tradition, therefore she says, 'I am not a Guru.'[40]

Spiritual Help

Question : When a serious enquirer is helped from the unknown quarters, is it the consciousness of enquirers who have lived before that helps the person or is it the Supreme Intelligence that helps the enquirer ?

Vimalaji: It seems possible that the unconsciousness or the conditioned energy of those by-gone enquirers can help a student of spirituality. Because the energy of, say, Jesus of Nazareth that was conditioned by manifesting in the physical body and living in it for 40, 50 or 80 years does not become unconditioned even when the person dies. The conditioned, individuated energy that manifested through those individuals should be existing in the earth, in the space, having a vibrational existence.

If the enquirer requires help and prays for help, perhaps those beings that have gone before, put on the forms, as you put on your coats or clothes; they put on the forms and come down to pat you on your shoulder and say, "Go ahead." It is a secret path and unless the enquirer has been extremely honest and has tried all his talents and gifts and has been through the tunnel of inner emptiness and nothingness, or in the dimension of Silence, I think the help is not received. As long as there is reliance on the I-consciousness, as long as there is reliance and trust on the mental effort, the cerebral effort, then the helps is not received. Unless you have emptied yourself completely from all identification with the known and you can stand stark naked before the cosmic life, you do not receive help.

As far as the Supreme Intelligence, the Cosmic Intelligence is concerned, it does not help. It cannot help, because help requires duality. The Receiver and the Giver. The Supreme Intelligence, the unconditioned Cosmic Consciousness is enfolded within you as it is unfolded in the Cosmos outside of you. It is within you and it may burst from within your being.

It may fill your being. That is not help. It is as if the Cosmic Energy, Cosmic Intelligence, Cosmic Consciousness gives itself totally unto you. As a lover gives himself or herself onto the beloved. It is the eradication of the illusory distance between the individual and the cosmic.

This help from without, from outside of you, is possible in relation to the liberated, enlightened persons that have gone before you. They can come and help you to dissolve and resolve your problems, point out how to get out of the rut in which you were stuck. The conditioned energy can take back the form in which it had existed on the earth and communicate with you. But the Cosmic Intelligence, the undifferentiated, unindividuated Cosmic Intelligence, being the essence of your being, may fill your being, but it does not help.

I wonder if I can clarify the difference between filling the being and eliminating duality and helping where the duality is still retained, sustained, maintained. For even after receiving help from outside, the serious religious or spiritual enquirer may find that the quality of his or her life and consciousness has not completely changed or been transformed.

When the emptied inner orbit of the serious enquirer gets filled with the unconditioned energy, when there is no I-ness but one-ness, when there is no sense of being somebody or something separate from the totality of Life, everything changes. The darkness of individual consciousness recedes as the darkness at dawn and the rays of the sun fill the consciousness and the night becomes the day.[41]

THE VARIOUS YOGAS

The science of yoga aims at establishing a contact between the individuated consciousness and the non-individuated, transcendental consciousness which is called Brahman. It presumes an omniscient trinity:

1) There is the transcendental principle of Life, which is indivisible, organic wholeness, which is called Brahman by Vedanta, Ishvara or Lord by Hatha Yoga and Purusha by Sankhya.

2) There is unindividuated, universal matter which is called Mula Prakriti by Hatha Yoga and Sankhya Yoga, and perhaps by other branches of Yoga, and Maya by Vedanta.

3) The third is: the individuated consciousness which is called *jiva* by Hatha Yoga and Raja Yoga and *pratyagatma* or reflected Brahman by Vedanta.

Hatha yoga tries to establish the contact between the individual and the transcendental consciousness by working upon the physical body. The physical body has all the energies that the universal matter or mula prakriti has. It has all the energies that the cosmic matter has. But the unified cosmic energies contained in that universal matter is diversified in the human body. The science of yoga shows us the way of gathering the distributed energies together, uniting the diversified energies and then educating them to function holistically instead of fragmentarily. Hatha Yoga uses the body. It uses the prana, the dynamic vital energy for disciplining and educating. Asanas (postures) and pranayama (controlled breathing) are the essence of hatha yogic discipline.

Hatha yoga uses the body as the instrument and with the help of the prana it awakens kundalini, the coiled up energy of prana at the base of the spine; and the awakening of the coiled up prana energy energises your whole being; energises your consciousness. The path is long; it is laborious. It consumes much time and energy.

Sankhya Yoga and Jnana Yoga focus all their attention and energies on the Purusha, the Purushottama, the Brahman. Prakriti is ignored, is neglected. The perfection of the Prakriti, the refinement or purification of the prakriti is not taken care of. Intellectual identification with the supreme Lord, the

Brahman, the Purushottama, is the essence of Sankhya Yoga, Jnana yoga, Vedanta, etc. Jnana yoga uses the cerebral organ, the faculty of will, the faculty of ideation and experiments in purifying, in uniting the diversified energies.

Bhakti yoga uses the emotional aspect of consciousness for uniting the energies, harmonising them through dedication and devotion to one point. The whole emotional energy is focussed on Ishvara and through the concentration of emotional energies, bhakti yoga tries to purify the physical and mental body.

Bhakti yoga utilises the emotional part and expounds the path of uniting with the supreme Brahman through emotional identification. The Supreme Lord is called by some the Father, the Beloved. Father, mother, child – all of these relationships are imagined and imposed upon the Purushottama, the Brahman and again Prakriti is neglected. The intoxication, the ecstasy of Bhakti in the life of Sri Ramakrishna Parahamsa or other such Indian saints created an imbalance on the physical level.

Karma yoga or the path of action uses the Prakriti or the mental body and the physical body. Through beneficial or good karmas towards the society in which a person lives, it wants to eliminate the separative ego consciousness. It is using thought power as well as the physical power.

Intellectual identification with the Purushottama, the Brahman and emotional identification with Ishvara, imposing and imagining a psychological relationship, is one aspect of some of the branches of Yoga.

Hatha yoga, tantra yoga and mantra yoga focus their attention on Prakriti. They focus their attention on the universal Prakriti, mula prakriti – the cosmic matter or the individuated prakriti in their bodies. They emphasise the matter and its energies contained in the body. With the help of prana energy, awakening kundalini and other psycho-physical powers occur. Mantra yoga manipulates the inner organs, their relationship and their energies with the help of sound energies. The sound energy can provoke the latent or dormant powers in your body. Manipulation of chakras also with bija mantras, with the help of very subtle sound, can provoke the latent energies contained and concealed in the human organs. Tantra Yoga manipulates the seven chakras in the body, the crucial and significant points where various nerves and arteries converge upon one another.

So through intellectual identification, emotional union and physical striving, [all these yogas] emphasise either the Purusha or the Prakriti. Raja Yoga is the only path where equal attention is paid to Ishvara, Prakriti and the individual ego – *jiva*.

The universal matter, the *mula prakriti* has individuated into a human body with a certain equilibrium. In the physical body there is a natural equilibrium and a natural harmony of energies. There is an equilibrium in the way they are dispersed and distributed for diversified functions, which is sufficient for our normal existence and relationships with people living in society, etc. But if you want to establish a contact with the highest, the transcendental, it will be an upward voyage. It will be an ascent. These energies and the equilibrium is useful for horizontal function relating to the orbit of the earth, relating to matter, to human structure. But if you want to take an ascending path, upward from matter and the energies contained in matter, towards the super sensory, supermental and super cosmic, that is transcendental, you have to create a new equilibrium in the physical. You have to create a new equilibrium in your mind or ordinary consciousness. Haha yoga helps you to create that new equilibrium through asana, *pranayama*, etc. and with the help of kundalini. And Raja Yoga helps you build up the new equilibrium through a master over your *chitta*, the repository in the consciousness, the ground of your consciousness.[42]

Intellectual knowledge, intellectual recognition, and even a limited realisation at the sensual and the mental level does not result in a new birth. That knowledge, recognition, that partial limited realisation, the flashes of reality through perception, through experience, do not transorm or transmute the physical frame, neither do they transform the energies contained in the mental frame. That is why both Hatha Yoga and Raja Yoga become necessary. The organisation of energies contained in the physical body and the rearrangement and reconditioning of energies contained in consciousness becomes necessary. The rearrangement and reorganisation of energies contained in the physical frame can be done through Hatha Yoga. But the re-arranging, re-organising of the mental energies, so that those energies are transformed into new energies, so that those mental energies shed all the limitations and conditionings imposed on them, is not attained through Hatha Yoga alone; even if you do *dharana*, the study of concentration, contemplation. That is why, after beginning with Hatha Yoga, one has to proceed with Raja Yoga.[43]

Raja Yoga

Among all the branches of yoga Raja yoga is called the king of yoga and the secret path indicated by Raja Yoga is called the sovereign path. It is thus called because it synthesises practically all the other branches of yoga, harmonises them, blends them together and creates a fascinating, majestic path for self-education and self-refinement for the evolution of a new equilibrium in the body, a new equanimity in consciousness, thus striving to perfect the physical body and the mental body given to a human being.[44]

Raja Yoga is the only path where equal attention is paid to Ishvara, Prakriti and the individual ego *(jiva)*. It is not purifying or refining one at the cost of the other. It is not deifying one at the cost of the other. It takes into its preview and compass all the three simultaneously, and this is the beauty, the uniqueness of Raja Yoga. In the sutra *Ishvara Pranidhanani* (Patanjali Yoga Sutra 11.1) and in the ninth chapter of the *Bhagavad Gita* verses 7 to 21, we have the surrendering of all actions to the Awareness that the unmanifest and the manifest are the dance of One and the same Brahman, same phenomenon, the same principle of sovereign Intelligence. Matter cannot be separated from Spirit, the Supreme Intelligence, and the Supreme Intelligence, the Lord, the Ishvara, the Brahman, can never be isolated from Prakriti, from matter – that is the basis of Raja Yoga.[45]

The science of Raja Yoga is a science of purification. You purify your biological organism and the psychophysical structure through Astanga Yoga (spiritual discipline). Then the growth culminates into the dimension of *samadhi*. The science of yoga cannot be limited to the practice of spiritual discipline or a little practice of concentration. It is a path of inner revolution, converting you from a fragmentary divided human being into the wholeness of your being.[46]

Organic wholeness of Life, interrelatedness of every being, of every expression of Life, and an intelligent harmony permeating the whole cosmos, these are the three discoveries of the Vedic and the Upanishadic period, upon which the science of Raja Yoga is based.[47]

This *raja-vidya, rajayoga,* this sovereign, supreme truth and the secret sovereign path which purifies your being is going to use not only the emotional part of you, not only the will power of your cerebral organ but *chitta*. Neither karma, nor bhakti, not jnana, nor dhyana, but it is going to focus its energies on *chittam,* the repository of all conditionings. It will not neglect the physical body – the asanas and the pranayama will accompany you on this path.

Thus the secret path is of purification of the centre of consciousness, the I-ness, the me-ness, the *ahamkara,* the ego consciousness which is the centre. Raja yoya says, don't tread on the periphery, don't use your emotions, dedicating them to someone, as in bhakti yoga; don't use your vital energy in action as in karma yoga; don't go on talking about abstract theories as in jnana yoga; instead tackle the centre.

The *chitta* in which the ego consciousness dwells, that is the point to be tackled. Raja yoga deals directly with the *chitta* and with the *ahamkara,* with the ego-consciousness, leaving aside the periphery.

It is called the supreme and sovereign path because it gives you the capacity of self-rule. Generally it is the impulses of the body that rule the mind. In a mentally evolved, knowledgeable person, the mind controls the physical impulses and yet rules the reason or rationality. The inheritance rules the conscious mind. The subconscious rules the conscious mind. The emotions overwhelm the reason and rationality. There is no self-rule. For some time you are governed and ruled by the impulses in the body, sometimes you are ruled and governed by even incompatible desires, contradictory wishes and aspirations. You are torn within.

It is called the prince of yoga, Raja vidya, king of vidya, king of knowledge, because it enables you for self rule. The body, the energies contained in the biological impulses, the mind with all the faculties and energies contained in mind voluntarily follow your inclinations, your intuition and your perception. You don't have to force them. They become voluntary companions. They become your elegant assistants.

If the ego enjoys the identification with the body and the mind, surely it is not going to correct it. It has not got the vitality to do it. So where is the source of vitality? Where is the source of the additional energy? There are two ways of having that vitality and energy. One is the path given to us by hatha yoga, asana and pranayama. Energising through asana and pranayama is one thing, and secondly allowing the mental movement to discontinue itself completely. Neither exercising the brain for new knowledge, nor exercising the mind for new experiences. It is the path of total relaxation. Not for one hour or two hours a day, but throughout the day – an inner relaxation. Relaxation energises. Relaxation of the whole body and abeyance of mental movement should be combined together. This is the secret path, pointed out by Krishna: a blending of Raja Yoga and Hatha Yoga together.[48]

Kundalini

Vimalaji in general avoided mention of Kundalini, even saying from time to time that it does not exist. It is possible that she avoided reference to Kundalini due to all the glamour which surrounds this word, and, wishing to emphasise that Kundalini is a physical result of a spiritual occurrence, she therefore preferred that people should not become enamoured with pursuing a physical goal. Kundalini should automatically 'rise' if the Truth is realized.

Vimalaji explained[49] that there are male and female energies in the person and these reside in the sex organs and the small of the back at the base of the spinal cord. With the help of prana energy, it is possible to give them an upward push and a vertical momentum. This is the physical aspect. Kundalini travels up to the lotus in the heart and, if development is normal, from thence to the throat centre and head centres:

> The sex energy had converted into individual or microscopic intelligence, energy of Intelligence [in the heart] with no division. The male-female division has disappeared now, the past-future-present division has disappeared, the knower and the known, the experiencer and the experience – all divisions and dualities have evaporated, in the process of that con-version into Intelligence. Now you have to still take one step further.

The same energy of prana, vital breath, is employed again to give an upward push or vertical velocity, vertical momentum to this individual intelligence, and take it to the crown of the head. So the individual intelligence... is now mingled with Brahman. The Atman has mingled with the Brahman. Up to the dimension of the heart it was *dhyanam*, meditation, but once that energy has reached the crown of the head, he calls it *samadhi*. It is a 'dimension'. No more an expression, no more a state of being, but a dimensional jump.[50]

The sex energy can be released for procreation, or it can be diverted, turned back from the sense organs, climbing gradually through the cavities, through the space right to the crown of the head:

That is possible when the purity of that energy, that creativity, that purity of the pranas has been retained. It is only the pranas that can become the carriers of that secretive subtle energy. Thought, conviction cannot help that energy to climb back, or to revert the process. Instead of procreation or recreation, it turns back to its source.

Vimalaji then further explained that the person who has deflected the energy of prana to the higher centres or chakras of the human body, due to purity of thought and purity of living, has a power to make that which he or she thinks become true. This is because the creative energy has reached the heart. When it reaches the throat, then whatever the person speaks becomes true, because that creative energy had made speech its abode.

When it travels up into the eyes, when it travels up to the Bhru Madyah – the point between the two brows– then the eyes become so powerful that the eyes can transfer the vitality to another human being, just through a glance. It might help you

understand the lives of Indian Yogis and the so-
called miracles ascribed to them. They are not miracles; they are the happenings of the inner subtle
world. So by a glance, the vitality, the creativity, is
transferred to another human being. It is a procreative energy, please let us remember that; but the
procreation is no more in the human form of flesh
and bone, it is on a subtler level that the procreation is taking place, transference of life is taking
place.[51]

*Vimalaji explained how a person with this energy can touch
an ill person and make him well, how, when this energy permeates the brain and the person's perception through the
eyes, it sees that there is a completion, a timelessness, a si-
multaneity which takes in birth, death, cause, effect in one
sweep. She explained that the Rishi said:*

You have two options. It is up to you whether you
use the energy as a procreative energy and bring
back another human being into the world, or turn
[the prana] back and bring it to the crown of your
head, travelling through all parts of the body, so the
transference of energy takes place on a subtler
plane, not only on the sensory level... When you
trace it back to its roots, when you trace everything back to its root, to its source, to its initial
cause, you go back to the Brahman, and therefore
to your existential essence. That Reality, that
Brahman, that Atman, the existential essence of a
human body, that creativity is identical with the
creativity of cosmic energy. The creativity of Brahman and there, you are the Brahman. You are the
reality.[52]

PART TWO

THE INNER REVOLUTION

1. INTRODUCTION

May you be blessed with this sustained seriousness of enquiry, with the urge to arrive at the unity of all the five layers of your life, and may you have the glimpses of that bliss in which your friend [Vimalaji] lives. It is not a privilege of the few, it is the consummation of human growth and it is within the reach of every human being who has the urge to learn, to discover and to live. [1]

The following three chapters explain in more detail the central core of Vimalaji's Teaching as it relates to the practice of enquiry (sadhana). Suffice it to say here that there are many paths to self-realisation, but the particular path which Vimalaji taught is based on Raja Yoga as expounded in the Yoga Sutras of Patanjali. She said that:

The teachings of Patanjali have a fascinating sweep and cover the whole life of the human race. His teachings contain the philosophy of perception, and the biology and chemistry of perception. He analyses the psychological structure of the human being and differentiates the universal mind stuff, common to the whole species from the individualised psychological structures built up by the human race through knowledge and experience. As an immaculate educationalist he tells us how the individualised mind can be educated and equipped with purity so that it merges back into the common mind stuff which has emerged as the process of mutation in the cosmic flow of nature.* He gives us the details of the process of purification for the physical organism, process of purification for the psychic structure and also indicates the nature, quality and modus operandi of the transformed human consciousness as a consummation of education.[2]**

This method involves the practice of self-observation, which eventually, through determined effort, results in the awareness of the different expressions of Purusha (the Divine Principles), as distinct from Prakriti-matter, our material bodies including the psyche. The indwelling Witness or Atma, or Godhead, becomes the See-er rather than the ego, which becomes externalized, and merely among the other viewed or witnessed objects. This is the 'inner revolution'.

---

* Each person has a psychic structure or soul which is their 'angel' or inner guru, the sat guru or gurudeva, which is consciousness and which guides the person through life after life. This psyche or soul is indeed consciousness or mind itself, but out of the plane or vast sea of universal consciousness, each individuated ring-pass-not of consciousness or soul has emerged to evolve. When the perfection of that individuated consciousness occurs through *sadhana* then the individual soul can merge back into the universal mind or consciousness.

** Self-realisation or Enlightenment is in fact an occurrence in the consciousness, soul or psyche of the individual when the consciousness itself realises its true nature. The soul or psychic structure must therefore itself undergo a process of evolution and the consummation of its education is its final dissolution into the universal consciousness, leaving the individuated Absolute in a pure form without any longer the need of an individual consciousness, because the Individuated Absolute is now directly in touch with the physical world, due to the sacrifice and self-evolution of the consciousness, the sat guru.

Vimalaji used the special words 'inner revolution', as a means of graphically and aptly describing the huge change in behaviour, perception and awareness which takes place when a human being 'returns to' (becomes or realizes) his or her Source, and views the world as the Divine Principle, the Ancient Witness, rather than through the eyes of a greedy, self-interested, egotistical body/mind. Vimalaji explained:

> a radical revolution is urgently needed before you can live as a human being... a psychological revolution has nothing to do with the collection of information ... it is concerned with a total change in your whole being. Knowledge about mutation, which is revolution, is not possible. Description of mutation through words is not possible... mutation is a total change through which you have to pass. You will have to break all the self-imposed and self-invented bondages. As you wake up from your sleep, so have you to wake up from disorder within you... Please be aware that no change in your pattern of psychical or mental behaviour can bring about a mutation. Right perception of every movement of life results in revolution.[3]

Living in Samadhi (translated by Vimalaji as the state of meditation) is the consequence of the dimensional shift which occurs in one's being due to the 'inner revolution'. According to Patanjali, the occurence of asamprajnata (beyond, unrelated to, knowledge) samadhi happens when there is:

> complete cessation of the movement of 'I'... the cessation of movement. In that *asamprajnata samadhi* there remains a consciousness that you are a human being, a member of the human species, not an individualised mind moving on the basis of knowledge... There is cessation of the movement of the individualised human mind and yet there is the samskara, the remnant of

beingness... so the universal common mind stuff emerging out of the mutation is still there.*⁴

Ultimately, even this slight trace of feeling you have a body will be transcended... The consciousness of being a human being, having a human body gets dissolved and what remains is the sense of the whole world, the whole cosmos. There is no sense of separateness, no sense of duality of you and the cosmos. It is a pure non-duality in the consciousness... With some individuals in one sweep of perception, the transcendence of the individualised mind takes place instantaneously. The perception and the transcendence or the transformation occur in one movement or in one flash of consciousness.

So there is only the sensation of life pulsating everywhere, without a sense of differentiation, without a sense of duality, without a sense of manyness... It is the consummation of the maturity and growth of consciousness.⁵

_____

After this revelation has occurred, the mind tends to convert it into a dead memory. But it is important to realise that revelation and the energy of Awareness left behind as the trace of that occurrence cannot be converted into experience, acquisition, achievement. This event, on the contrary, must become

_____

* There are many grades and levels of samadhi, ranging from a sense of the Void which is also combined with a sense of being a person in the world, right through to the 'level' or state of being where the Individuated Absolute is not even aware of the existence of the physical plane of this world. Vimalaji is here describing an intermediate state of samadhi in which the person is aware of him or herself as a Void endless stretching, whilst at the same time, the universal consciousness which is connected with time and space is still extant.

stabilized in the levels and layers of the human being. The flash of revelation does not in itself cause the holistic transformation of the body. That Energy must be stabilized and incorporated into the energy bodies of the being. For this, three requirements are necessary: *tapa* (unity of movement of brain, mind and senses, *dama* (voluntary withdrawal by the mind from the sense objects, and karma (living the life of action in which the actions are in harmony with responsibilities which arise during the various phases of one's life). Then and only then the revelation stabilizes in your life.

Life has a double movement: that of knowing and being in the state of non-knowing, that of doing and being in the state of non-doing, that of relationship and of solitude, that of speech and of silence. These two dimensions are woven into each other as the darkness of the night and the light of the day are woven together. They are not contradictory to each other. They nourish each other.[6]

The individual 'inner revolution' will take place by gradual refinement and improvement of all levels and layers of being, the physical, emotional, mental and psychological dimensions of existence, for these components of a human being must be purified sufficiently to be able to perceive Intelligence, the Cosmic Movement. When this dimensional shift, this 'inner revolution' occurs, after a longer or shorter period of intense self-discipline and spiritual inquiry, we understand ourselves to be something utterly different from an ego in a body, using a mind.

Vimalaji's Inner Revolution is not a quest to be entered upon out of curiosity or personal ambition or desire for occult experiences. On the contrary, the purpose of self-transformation is to fulfill one's human destiny, to understand what one IS, that we are little Gods, condensed Cosmos, and we have the ability to bring about transformation of life on Earth, instead of plundering, war and exploitation of the natural world, the animals, forests and seas. By becoming what we truly are, we can contribute towards the completed perfection of the universe.

Vimalaji did not say like certain jnanis, 'this world is non-existent and therefore why bother about it? You just have to realize that all this manifestation is but a dream.' Vimalaji recognized some kind of reality of the manifested world; even if ultimately the world is impermanent, changeable and mutable, and thus not the Reality, even if the world is a dream, let us make it a better dream, not a nightmare! For the material world in which we happen to have appeared with consciousness can be modified and perfected through the Energy of Love, once that Energy has been realised, and then it will become a paradise. Such a destiny is in the hands of humanity, and according to Vimalaji, the outcome will be positive.

In the silence, every pore of your being is relaxed, which results in the openness and receptivity of the consciousness contained in the body. Then the interaction between the cosmic energy of Intelligence (Chiti Shakti) and the individual energy of awareness *(chetana)* takes place. It is in that interaction, that non verbal communion, the effortless communion, that dimensional transformation takes place. In the movement of relationship a dynamic change comes about and in the moments of unconditional relaxation and magnificent emptiness of silence, the dimensional transformation gets the opportunity to occur, to materialise.

So we work on both fronts: in the midst of relationship and in the sacredness of aloneness. Both are supplementary and complementary to each other. Then relationships themselves open the door to freedom. They awaken the energy of love and compassion. And in the silence of aloneness, the austerity of renunciation wakes up and dawns upon the heart.

The last illusion of separation from the cosmic life is this deeply rooted feeling: I am somebody, I am an entity, I have an identity, which has to be protected, for whose survival I have to work. The last illusion of separation, which means really fragmentation of the wholeness of Life, that illusion is exploded. When renunciation reigns supreme in your being, then you move around, wherever life brings you, in an unassuming manner. You live like a rose flower by the roadside. It is fulfilled in blooming and blossoming and you are fulfilled in uncovering, unfolding the contents of freedom, love and peace through your presence and through your interaction with others if and when necessary.[7]

The movement from ignorance to understanding takes place in a split second. It is a timeless happening. You create an idea of time around it. You say I have understood it literally, verbally, academically: now I must practise it. Truth need not be practiced. It has to be lived. There is a difference between practicing and living. In practice you repeat and in living there is no repetition. It seems to me that psychologically there is ignorance and understanding. Understanding causes mutation. The belief in the slow process, the gradual process, is something unscientific.

One has to be in the eternal timeless present and live the truth that one understands, immediately instantaneously. If the truth is allowed to go back to memory and remain there unlived, unimplemented, then it will go on fermenting with much untruth or falsity collected in the memory. It loses its vitality, it loses its dynamism.

For a psychological mutation to take place, it is vitally necessary that we learn to live the truth that we understand immediately, without worrying about 'What will be the price? What will be the consequences?' Religious revolution requires the fearlessness to meet the consequences of freedom.[8]

2. SELF-OBSERVATION

Although Vimalaji did recommended a particular practice she did not like it to be called either a technique or a method, due to the fact that it could become dogmatised, rigidified and then misunderstood. Her recommendation for the practice of self-observation, as a first step in stilling the mind, was in essence a re-presentation of Raja Yoga in modern words for Westerners. Vimalaji was the first to stress that it is one path among many, albeit a very direct way, of realising the 'Multi-dimensional Wholeness' or Isness of life. However, she warned against potentially dangerous practices:

> Any technique or method that provokes or stimulates the chemistry of the body is dangerous. As techniques of awakening kundalini force – because it is a physical force – are very dangerous, even *shaktipat* or transmission of psychic power from teacher to student can be very dangerous. I have come across thousands of young men and women who met with nervous breakdowns because their bodies were not capable of assimilating the newly stimulated energy and its frequency. Any technique that stimulates or provokes the psycho-physical energy suddenly, abruptly is dangerous. I call it raping the psyche. It is a rape of the psyche, like the psychedelic drugs.[1]

Self-observation, observing oneself, can begin on a simple level by simply watching one's behaviour, so that one becomes aware of the way in which one functions as a personality, and one begins to see the many faults and failures and stupidities of one's prejudiced, unconscious life. But

*watching your behaviour is simply a first step. There is
something more intense that is required. It involves sitting
quietly, alone, comfortably, and simply watching your mind.*

*It sounds so simple but actually it is extremely difficult.
Whilst carried on at the level of mind it requires constant,
minute by minute effort until the breakthrough is achieved.
The thoughts bubble everywhere; they come hurling from
outside into the field of one's own mind, a veritable mass of
colour and vibration. As one struggles, not through concentration, but through observation, not through violently
forcing anything upon the mind, but by gently learning to
identify thoughts as 'something other' coming from 'outside'
there are brief moments of absence of thoughts, which gradually through practice, extend themselves.*

*One may need to go away for a period of weeks or months to
intensely practice. Not all people are suited to do it. As
Vimalaji said, 'Some people cannot stand it.' There is a fine
balance between the different fields of consciousness, which
when disturbed can result in schizophrenia, ADD, or many
other mental disturbances There is a time in a person's life
when they are ready to proceed, but it should not be forced,
and there should be a Teacher watching the enquirer, should
anything untoward start to develop.*

*Concurrently with practicing self-observation, one should be
working on getting rid of attachment and desires in daily life,
for all levels, all layers of the individual must be purified so
as to become receptive to the finer vibrations of the "higher"
aspects of Life.*

We have to learn to observe, that is to say, we have to educate our psychological structure to remain in the beauty, the
sensitivity of attention. To sustain that and no get victimised
by the habit of judging and reacting, requires tremendous
patience.[2]

We educate ourselves to sit quietly and watch whatever comes up in the mind, without reacting to what is seen. If there is reaction-free observation, in a short time the movement of thought subsides by itself. That is, if the thoughts fails in attracting your notice, in compelling you to react, then they subside. This is the procedure towards the state of meditation.[3]

The difficult part comes of educating the mind and the brain to voluntarily discontinue its movement in every direction. [The mind] does not give up easily its addiction to motion. One requires tremendous patience with the cerebral organ which has been sharpened. So when you sit down with yourself or spend some days with yourself, you notice that immeasurable velocity, that tremendous, fantastic momentum with which the thoughts come and go, the emotions come, the memories come up and the Seer has to be there just seeing it, not looking at it. Looking is the activity of the monitor, the 'I', the 'me', the mind. Seeing is the energy principle of your life. It is an involuntary action. The seen energy is not unlimited; it is vast, it is gigantic, but it has had a beginning and it can have an end. When the seen, that is the past, the known, the conditioned, gets exposed to that seeing energy, it gets exhausted. Looking is an activity, it is a joint activity of the mind and the optical nerves; but seeing is unrelated to that which is seen, because one did not want to see it. It is there, therefore it is seen.[4]

I wonder why looking simply becomes such a problem... Out of habit I get carried away [by thought] or I am carried away for a fraction of a second, and then suddenly I become aware, 'goodness me, I was carried away', so I come back. You come back to the state of observation. [You can] watch even the process that I am getting carried away and have come back. Then the frequency of being carried away will be lessened, the duration of the period of being carried away will decrease. And if there is the intensity of enquiry and if there is spending reasonable amount of time in learning how to observe, I think one gets over this obstacle of the deep-rooted habit.[5]

We are in such a hurry that instead of observing and watching, we would like some technique, formula and method to change it [the dimension of consciousness] quicker. We feel that observation does not give us any experiences. The movement of the past goes into abeyance while we are observing, because it is a non-reactional attentiveness. While in concentration we get extrasensory perceptions and non sensual experiences. We are attracted by them. Though we want transformation, mutation or inner revolution intellectually, emotionally we are craving for some new experiences... We feel that those experiences will change us, [but they] might condition us.[6]

The body is steady, we abstain from verbal speech and close the eyes, so that the contact with the outer world is no longer there. You are now alone with the inner life pulsating in you. You do not see the outer objects and then you see something else. You notice that though there is no voluntary effort to think, thoughts are moving. The movement of thought structure is independent of your volition. Do you see what a tremendous discovery it can be? The discovery that what I call my thoughts, my feelings, my memory, have a movement and a momentum independent of me, this discovery has a dual effect. One, the pride and vanity that 'I think', that these are 'my thoughts', that vanity disappears... [and] a humility comes about. Secondly whenever the thoughts came up, I acted upon them. First I called them mine and secondly I gratified their needs. [Now] there is a new relationship coming up: I look at them not to judge, not to accept or reject them, not to act upon them, not to change them; I just look at them. I look at the trees, I look at the sunshine, I look at the clouds; and in the same way I look at the movement of thoughts in utter freedom. There is no pressure on me to do anything with those thoughts – to suppress, to repress, to change. So there is a space between the movement of thought structure and a part of thought structure that was calling itself 'I'. The marvellous thing is, when you look at the thoughts in simplicity, not claiming them, not rejecting them, they lose their grip on you.[7]

If you learn to observe and watch thought process without any reaction, any value judgment, then you will see it is a repetitive, mechanical movement; it does not belong to you. There is movement of thought, but you are not the thinker; there is movement of knowledge, but you are not the knower. It is a movement that is going on incorporated in the psychophysical structure; it goes on on its own, so it is not necessary to identify with that movement. The non-identification will lessen the misery and the psychological suffering.[8]

Thoughts cannot be excluded. The momentum of the thinking process lies in the act of identification. When you watch the thoughts without identifying yourself with them, one thought comes up and wanders about for some time; finding that there is no one to reject or accept it, the mind hops over to another thought. There also, it finds that there is no one to select and reject, and it goes to a third.

Watch it as you watch a child playing. You don't condemn. You don't try to discipline. You don't try to control. Every attempt to control the mind gives it double momentum to run away from you... When you see the thoughts coming up, you will see that the momentum is exhausted by itself.[9]

When you look at the thoughts in simplicity, not claiming them, not rejecting them, they lose their grip on you. And when there is that relationship of unconditional freedom between the movement of thought structure and the observer, a very funny thing happens. You feel inwardly as if you are sitting in front of a mirror and you are looking at yourself. You realise that all those thoughts, memories, experiences, preferences, prejudices, conclusions, they are you and you are not separate from them. The reflection in the mirror and you, are the same. The tremendous momentum had created an illusion of a separate thinker, a separate looker and observer, but they are the same. The thinker and the thought are not separate.[10]

In the beginning one is conscious that, I am observing. The mind, the monitor, the I-consciousness, is trying to educate itself. So it is very conscious, but gradually, progressively, when the state of observation is allowed to get settled in the neurochemical system, that self-consciousness of the ego centre melts away... Education in observation results in a state where there is no observer...The observation is still there. Only the self-centred observer, who was posing as the watcher, the observer, the perceiver, has retraced the step and gone into abeyance. It is not destroyed, because that product of the human civilization is very useful for functioning on the physical level.[11]

Self-observation leads to the state of Silence

Observation leads to the cessation of the mental movement. First the flame of attention becomes steady, and then the consciousness that we are observing also disappears. There is neither the observer nor the observation, and silence reigns supreme in the consciousness of the person. The realm of words, ideas, thoughts, symbols is left behind. We are standing at the frontiers of the known and the horizons of the unknowable are before us... Observation leads to an inner silence. There is no more centre, the 'I' at the centre saying to itself, 'I am observing', but the flame of attentiveness permeates the whole being... there is nothing like subconscious and unconscious for that person. It has become one homogeneous whole for him, with no compartments any more. Throughout the day, whatever the person does and whatever happens to the person is observed quietly by that flame of attentiveness, and therefore no possibility of dreams, tensions, conflicts.[12]

In the state of observation there is a movement without the observer and without the observing, no centre making the conscious effort to observe. That was necessary while we were learning to observe. Once it is learnt, then efforts become irrelevant, spontaneously it goes on. As there is nothing to observe and there is no one at the centre making conscious efforts to observe, there is silence. Silence is being without a centre, without making a conscious effort in any direction whatsoever. There is no possibility of experiences in the dimension of Silence.[13]

In the beginning the consciousness that 'I am observing' is there. 'I am observing. I have seen this. I have noticed that.' But when the state of observation is sustained and you go back to it time and again in your daily life, then that state of observation takes place like inhalation and exhalation of breath takes place... If the state of observation without the 'I', without the one being conscious that it is observing, is sustained, and the contents of the mind are thus observed, (they being finite and not unlimited), they subside and do not interfere any more... So what remains is an ocean of Silence.[14]

Though the contents of the subconscious and the unconscious may be vast, they are limited. They are not without beginning or end. A person who spends time in quiet observation comes to a phase when nothing more is exposed, there is nothing more to be observed. Therefore the observer also disappears. The observer was created by me voluntarily in order to learn observation. It was a voluntary division created by me. It had only a conceptual reality. Now there is no observer and nothing is exposed for observing; there is what I call Silence.[15]

3. THE DIMENSION OF SILENCE

Silence is the non-action of the ego.
Silence is the total relaxation of
the ego, the self, the me.

'Silence' is one of the most important and most frequently used words in Vimalaji's Teaching. If thoughts can be stopped, not through force, but by learning to refuse to allow their entry into the field of mind, then the chitta, or mind-stuff, will not be shaken and noise and vibrations will not be present to prevent the mirroring or transference to a dimensional shift which is 'higher' and 'above' and 'beyond' the (taken as) normal functional dimension of the human mind. The chitta, being still, becomes a clear pool so that the energy field of the abstract mind comes into operation.

One means of stopping the flow of thoughts (among many different practices) is the method of self-observation, as discussed in the previous chapter. If the mind can actually watch the mind, in a sense temporarily dividing itself into two parts, then it can be seen that the thoughts are a phenomenon almost as physical, and certainly as transitory, as other physical phenomena. Prayer, devotion, trust in God, and self-observation (and also other practices such as breath control, etc.) are all means to an end, that is, the stopping of thoughts outside the ring-pass-not of the individual, or individuated mind, so that the mind ceases its activities and noise, and becomes a clear mirror which can reflect the Reality, or more correctly, the Reality can express Its true Self through the instrument of the mind. Vimalaji prefers to use the word 'individuated' when describing the chitta or mind-stuff, or field of energy within the ring-pass-not of a particular ego or personality. This is because 'individuated' implies that some of the universal chitta has become 'trapped' or confined in an individuated field, although it is still a continuum of the infinite energy field, the Cosmic Consciousness. It is held magnetically by the individual point of consciousness within the endless Consciousness.

Thus, in the state of silence, instead of looking through the two eyes as a human being, we start to see the world firstly through the awakened soul or jivatma which is temporarily oneself. This soul could be said to be the form of expression of the Formless Monad or Spirit, and is a small spark of the infinite Soul, Paramatman. If we look at the world as a Soul rather than through human eyes, then we see the same visual images but with a completely different understanding because a different 'organ' is perceiving.

It is in the state of Silence that the individual ego gets annihilated, not through vanishing, but through being swamped, infiltrated, usurped, engulfed in the unending endlessness of one of the layers or 'planes' of Cosmic Consciousness.

This is not an event, not an experience, not a single, defined happening, but a series of expansions of understanding, which come about through a directed, individual, determined quest, an enquiry, sadhana. Like a determined dog following the scent of its master, the psyche sniffs out the next 'step', the next moment of understanding, and, as each understanding reveals itself, it becomes apparent that it was always there, and always understood, but needed only to be recognised.

Silence, therefore constitutes a range of vibratory perceptions which occur in stages:

1) When thoughts stop pestering the mind, the state of individual Observer is attained. There is a dimensional shift,

2) Awareness of the Fire, the Intelligence, the Wholeness is felt,

3) An understanding of what constitutes this Intelligence is developed by the individual Witness,

4) *This Intelligence may be felt as a Unicity, an occupying Presence, a vibration in the muscles and body, and bones. This expression of Brahman, the Cosmic Consciousness, the Supramental Consciousness,
is known or perceived as an all-permeating, unlimited,
infinite, omniscient, omnipresent Energy or vibration,*

5) *Whereas before, there was the effort of the mind in
learning to turn away thoughts, now there is no effort.
There is an automatic response. More than that, the
Presence is always there, and it requires only the recognition, the awareness of the Presence, in order to
feel it.*

6) *Eventually, the consciousness, which feels unified
with the Presence, realises that it is the Presence the
Seer.*

The Cosmic Movement or One Unicity is felt in the physical
body as a physical vibration, in the astral body as pure love,
and in the mind body as Awareness, that is, what Vimalaji
calls Silence, which is the feeling of being outside or above
oneself, of looking down from above the head onto the world
and onto oneself, a feeling of expansion and interconnected-
ness. But perhaps this state of Silence or awareness has even
further to expand horizontally so that the barrier of the individual being aware is finally broken, and there is no individual to be aware, hence resulting in a Self-awareness where
the Self knows itself to be everything, and outside and beyond
even the state of Silence.

To attain the state of Silence, a person has to want it more
than any other thing. If and only if the person wants it
beyond everything else, will it be attained. It requires a great
determination and dedication. A few hours here or there
once or twice a week, thinking of God, is not sufficient. It
must be a total and complete commitment in one's life. It
requires 'prayer without ceasing.' It requires a willingness to
relinquish everything and anything to attain the goal.

It should be understood very clearly that silence does not mean void or emptiness; that silence does not imply paralysis of action. Silence of mind is a dimension of life which has its own momentum. Forcibly silencing the mind is not arriving at real silence. If I chant, repeat certain words, and allow the biochemical effect of sound-vibrations to act upon me, an artificial state of peace can be created. If I take drugs like LSD, psilocybine or mescaline, a temporary expansion of the consciousness takes place. You can stimulate such artificial states of your being. I am not referring to that. Silence arrived at through violence, suffocation or suppression, is not silence.[1]

The mind does not get silenced. By its very nature, the mind is restless. People are trying hard to stimulate an experience of silence. If I go to a cave, if I sit there for hours, or for weeks or months, and I have cut myself off from every manner of activity, and the senses are not in touch with the objective reality, the mind has no scope to move outward and it may experience a silence. But it is a dead silence. There is no life in silence which is experienced in isolation from human relationships. Silence comes to life as a dimension only when you are living with people.[2]

It should be clearly understood that till the experience of Silence or Emptiness takes place, mental movement does exist. Mind and its movement do get refined by the touch of the Silence, but till the discontinuity of mental movement there cannot be even the feel of Silence or Emptiness. The ISNESS exists in its pristine glory, beyond words and beyond even imagination.[3]

The human mind with the help of thought constructs space-time sections... It has to transcend its own thought, intellect and senses, or in other words, the mind has to negate the experiencer, the observer, the thinker, through understanding. When the thinker is negated, there is total silence of the mind.

So you allow the mind to relax. You look at it, watch it, you don't touch it. And when you do not touch your reflection, when you do not touch the movement, then the movement loses its vitality; it subsides on its own. Silence is a tension and pressure-free state of your being.[4]

The I-consciousness is not moving. It moves when you want to acquire something from someone, when you want to acquire pleasure. When you do not want to acquire anything, when you do not want to react, then naturally the 'I', the 'me', the contrived, conditioned structure which we have inherited, goes into non-action. Silence is the non-action of the ego. Silence is the total relaxation of the ego, the self, the me.

Non-action of the ego, going into abeyance of the self, the me, the I-consciousness, is really non-action of the total past contained in me, non-continuation of acquired knowledge and experience. Now that movement comes to an end. This is what we call Silence. It is not meditation yet, but it is Silence. Discontinuity of the movement of knowledge, experience and inheritance, is silence.[5]

Just to take the plunge into the ocean of inner silence becomes a terrible difficulty with the modern individual because he feels he lives for his own doing... Surrendering all activities, surrendering the sense of the actor, the experiencer, the observer, the humility of faith in one sweep carries an enquirer into the ocean of Silence.[6]

The I-consciousness, the ego that had gone voluntarily into discontinuity jumps back. It wants to claim and say, 'I have had an experience of silence.' The 'I' can never have that experience; the 'I' can have an experience of quietness, of abstinence from speaking, it can have experience of non motion; but silence is something which cannot be experienced.

For the mutation to take place, the silence has to crystallise. It is only when the silence crystallises as the normal dimension of consciousness that the mutation, the quantum jump into the state of *dhyanam* occurs. It is not the result of any human effort. It occurs if this period of being merged into or being immersed into the ocean of Emptiness is gone through.[7]

The impact of the state of Silence : powers and energies

In the state of Silence new powers are activated and the individuated being may become a person with tremendous charisma and talents. But for the next expansion to occur, one must keep a deep sense of humility and sacrifice in the realisation that these talents and psychic powers are another form of maya, of distraction.

In the Silence moves the Cosmic mind. In Silence moves the conditionings of the five elements.* So there is subtle movement even in Silence. The conditioned mind of the person has gone into abeyance. It is in the ocean of inner space. That space is full of cosmic movement, call it a universal Intelligence that is moving there, call it Cosmic Intelligence that is moving there.[8]

[When] the seen and the seeing energy subside into their sources, there is *maunam* or silence or emptiness. So the seeing and the seen are replaced by infinite silence of emptiness. It is still tougher to be in that state, if at all a *sadhaka* has patience and humility to be in that state. Nothing happens,

---

* This means that in the all-permeating expression of Reality various unseen energies are moving, including the five elements of fire, water, earth, air, ether, from which the material world is shaped.

no experiences, you come out of silence after 2 or 3 hours and somebody asks you, "What were you doing?"

– I don't know, nothing.

– But you were sitting there with your closed eyes for 3 hours, what happened?

– Nothing.

– What did you get out of it?

– Nothing.[9]

So, people feel lost, because nothing happens. Nothing happens to whom? To their sense of separate I-ness. Nothing happens to them as a separate entity. From all divisions, they have gone back into their wholeness. Even the subject/object division, the I, the me, the not-me, all that disappears. So this dissolution, this temporary dissolution of the sense of division, of the sense of separateness, is felt like death and people are frightened. It is not the death of the ego. It is not the destruction of the ego. It is only that the centre, the ego, as the centre of consciousness, has become non-operative. A different dimension of consciousness is coming up. But it takes time.

People are afraid of silence. People are afraid when there is emptiness of silence within. If by any good luck their mental movement goes into abeyance, they feel suffocated, because we are used to the movement of thought, of an idea, of a word. We are used to tension, pressure. And when the mental movement stops, there is a holistic relaxation; nothing happens, nothing moves, and the person used to the movement, used to the sound or the tension of a thought, feels lost. 'I don't know what is happening to me.' Why must 'you' know what is happening? Let it happen. We want to interpret. We want to analyse the experiences, measure their religiosity. [10]

The conditioned mind and the brain stop moving, and you find yourself surrounded by emptiness. No thoughts, no feelings, no sentiments, nothing. That is an auspicious moment. One has to be in that silence fearlessly. The mind raises question at the first touch of silence. The Ego gets frightened because it does not see any direction to go, any work to do, any thoughts to think. But at that moment of total silence one has to have faith in Life and surrender oneself in the lap of that silence, as a small child relaxes in the lap of its mother. It is only then when we relax in that silence completely that the energy contained in that silence begins to manifest. This non-material, non-cerebral energy was called by Sri Aurobindo Supramental Consciousness, by Vinoba Universal Consciousness, by Ramakrishna Mother Kali. This energy becomes available to us the moment we surrender our vanity and pride our knowledge and experience at the altar of silence.[11]

So [there must be] an urge to find out what is beyond the brain, beyond the mind and to merge in the ground Reality, the existential Essence. Then, passing through the tunnel of emptiness, this tunnel of silence, seems to be a necessary phase. It is not the destination. Because if you allow that silence, that total relaxation, that wholeness of the being, to remain there, as an operative dimension, then really many powers do get developed in that dimension. Then comes about an extraordinariness, a magnetic quality to the person. And unless there is the urge, the deep urge for union with the ultimate Reality and one has no curiosity about the powers, one is not tempted for using them for any purpose whatsoever, then only those powers that develop in silence also subside, as the thought movement subsides at the mental level.[12]

Silence of the totality of mind is a dimension of life which is not yet explored by us. I can assure you that silence is a hundred times more powerful and dynamic than eloquence, than all the languages of the world put together. The momentum of silence is tremendous. The explosion of silence, when it takes place within a human being, brings about a radical revolution.[13]

In a silent mind, the Unmanifest, the Immeasurable, the Unknown, the Timeless, the Truth, the unconditioned conscious Energy, self-expresses itself as it is self-existent and self-consistent.

If one allows oneself to be in the dimension of silence, then the energy of intelligence or Awareness, the energy that is born of the non-duality of silence begins to vibrate in the body.[14]

On the physical level there is a kind of double functioning – thought and non-thought– and then there is the dimension of pure awareness which is activated by the abeyance, the non action, the silence, the meditation or whatever you call it. There seems to be an ascendance and education helps in that ascendance –instincts, intuition, thought consciousness, knowledge and awareness. Awareness is a very subtle energy like the energy of perfume. You stand near a rose plant and you feel the perfume. The eyes see the flower and you feel the perfume. So like the energy of the perfume, the energy of awareness emanates from the person, you feel it.[15]

The state of observation then becomes a normal dimension of consciousness. So there is freedom from the clutches of the past, the clutches of the known... Tremendous energy is released in that freedom. In that silence of freedom, in the relaxation of freedom, the latent energies which were not tapped by the human race, conditioned or channelled up till now, like the energy of love, like the energy of peace, like the energy of compassion, of freedom, those energies get activated in every drop of your blood. They were there but we were busy with something else.[16]

So what happens in the dimension of silence? When you get moments of leisure, when you sit down, relax and plunge yourself into that dimension of silence, that dimension of healing energies, then Intelligence or perceptive sensitivity gets activated in the body. Meditation is a state of consciousness which has a perceptive Intelligence. The content is not thought, knowledge, memory, experience. The content is the emptiness of silence which is full of Intelligence. In India they call it *Atman, Paramatman.* Let us call it Intelligence. Thought is intellect, which is a cerebral energy. Thought is an energy created by the past inheritance. Impulse is a biological energy. Intelligence is an energy born of the emptiness of Silence, of the space of silence.[17]

When thought does not move, when emotions do not move, when there is no pressure on the nervous system or the chemical system, when there is that holistic relaxation, complete relaxation, then the curative and healing energies in the body began to move. Does not that happen when you sleep? When you sleep profoundly even for two hours without dreams, when the mind does not move, then rejuvenation, refreshment, recreation of cells in the body take place. It is the relaxation that has healing energies. It is relaxation that activates the creative energies, the healing energies... [and this] takes place in the dimension of silence.[18]

For those who live in silence, the scars of stress and strain are healed. The damages done by the stress and strain of life are repaired. That is the first impact noticeable for the utilitarian mind which asks, 'What is the advantage of meditation, what is the result of meditation?' It seems to me that nothing heals like silence, if it is not converted into an experience of mind and if we do not try to suck pleasure out of it... the healing begins to take place as if one is getting reborn. We are talking about a psychic mutation.

In profound sleep your whole body, your whole being receives the energy from the cosmos; the cosmic energy operates while you are relaxing. In the same way in the state of awakening when your psycho-physical movement or thought movement goes into abeyance, the cosmic intelligence operates upon your being in that relaxation. When you were sleeping it had worked upon you, but you were passive then. Now it works upon you while you are awake. That is the fusion of universal energy and the energy encased in a human body – individual energy.[19]

In the cessation of mental activity, in the cessation of all activity of the conditioned mind, the action of the Cosmic and the Universal takes place. We are no more in the dimension, in the prison house of individual consciousness, but like the drop in the ocean, the individual consciousness has merged itself into the Whole, into the cosmic, the universal. That is what the Sufis call the mystical marriage of the individual and the universal.[20]

4. MEDITATION

In the state of Silence the awakened soul remains aware of Itself as individual observer. In this dimension,the personality, now connected with the Soul becomes aware of itself as an unseparated Energy of Intelligence within the Universal Consciousness, the Cosmic Consciousness. This is the state of meditation, dhyan. If this dimension of consciousness is sustained and 'settles down' – 'the inside adjusting to the outside' – the individuated experiencer realises, 'I am That':

It is important to understand that these descriptions are words only, and that the Cosmic Mind Itself, of which the enlightened being is an undivided part, also consists of 'planes' or Energy Fields of Consciousness of varying vibratory and magnetic capacities; and thus the being sails in a sea incomprehensible and mysterious, differentiated but united, interpenetrating microwaves, particles, beams of light, fields of force, wavelengths, matter and anti-matter, known and unknown.

What is meditation ?

The word meditation in the English language has one meaning and a quite different meaning in oriental languages. The English word 'meditation', derived from the root 'to meditate', implies a person who is the meditator and a subject or a theme upon which the person meditates. To meditate is to reflect and to analyse. It is an activity of the mind, to contemplate.

So, there is a meditator, there is the activity of meditating, and there is the state of reflection or contemplation, which is called meditation. [In the East], *dhyanam* is a way of living, an alternative way of living, not merely an activity of the brain, of the mind.[1]

Meditation is not an activity at all. It is a revolution in the perspective of life, and in the way of living. May I say it is an entirely new way of living?[2] Meditation is a way of living where relationships are movements of relaxation and not tensions and pressures.[3]

Meditation cannot be taught. It is a way of living which everyone has to learn by oneself. It is a holistic way based on an holistic perspective of Cosmic Life. Sitting in silence is helpful only to quieten the mind and put the body in a steady position. You cannot sit in meditation as it is entirely unrelated to the physical posture. It cannot be practised because it is not a psychological or cerebral movement. It is living in a non-structural, non-patternistic, spontaneous way... Meditation cannot be socialised. It is neither individual nor group activity. It is transformation in the content of human consciousness as well as the dynamic of human relationships.[4]

When the individual touches the Infinite for the first time, a process of adjustment begins which is effortless, in the sense that Awareness (as distinct from consciousness of the ego) is ever-present and beyond the mind. It is the supervision of the mind by the ego which involves effort, but once the barrier between the individuated cosmos and the Universal Divinity has been dissolved, then on this level of perception, which does not involve the senses or the mind, it becomes an effortless awareness.

Up to *dharana*, techniques, methods are necessary... Meditation, *dhyana*, is for the transportation of consciousness into thought-free, time-free, world-free reality, because after *dhyana* is *samadhi*... *Dhyana* is the ending of all techniques and methods. *Dhyana* is the ending of the concept that you can transform further. You have tried your level best from *yama, niyama* to *dharana*. So meditation is the phase in which the last effort is to be made, and that last effort is to be effortless and to be methodless, to be techniqueless. The last effort is to put your whole being in the lap of the cosmic energy as it were...

When you go to sleep, you don't make an effort, you relax unconditionally. You have so much faith in sleep which causes complete forgetfulness, you are not afraid of sleep. No effort, no clinging to the centre of the 'me' or 'not-me'... The only difference between sleep and *samadhi* is that in sleep there is no awareness except for a Yogi. In meditation there is the same unconditional relaxation, total relaxation and complete elimination of the centre of the 'me'... If you try to make an effort to sleep, you won't sleep, you'll waste the night in efforts; so there is a dimension of effortlessness which is also a dimension of Life. Effort is one dimension and effortlessness is another. Is there any effort in love? Is there any effort in the majesty of innocence? That is why in Silence also there is no effort, not because we do not appreciate the significance of methods and techniques, but they have no relevance here.

So relax into an unconditional effortlessness and let the life operate upon you. Your effortlessness does not mean a void or a blankness or a darkness or an inertia. Please do see this. Meditation is not a state of inertia, it is not a state of passivity, it is not a state of mere void; but when you thus relax unconditionally, you relax totally, then the supreme Intelligence operates.[5]

Meditation is the essence of spirituality. You do not have to do anything but to educate your physical organism and psychological structure to move into non-action gracefully, voluntarily and see what happens in that state of non-action. Once there is that state of non-action or silence or stillness, then things happen by themselves. It is cosmic Intelligence that takes over the charge of our being.[6]

Meditation begins where the realm of duality ends. It is a state of awareness in which there is no experiencer to take any experience. Meditation is not a capacity of the mind. Total silence opens the door to meditation.[7]

When your being is not divided into the observer and the observed, the seer and the seen, the doer and the act, or the experiencer and the experienced, when your being and all the faculties contained in you do not divide themselves as subject and object, then in that undivided existence of yours, in that virgin unity of your being, the mystery, the secret gets revealed unto you; you cannot know it, you cannot measure it but it gets revealed unto you. It is only when all the outgoing activities have spontaneously gone into abeyance that the revelation can occur, can happen.[8]

Dying to the past is another word for meditation. Dying to that part of activity of your consciousness which has been conditioned, through centuries. Not the whole consciousness has been conditioned. There is a part of the brain, there is a part of consciousness which is not conditioned. The front lobe of the human brain is not yet discovered. It is like a virgin land and man has not been able to identify anything in this part of the brain. Dying to that part of the brain which has been conditioned, thereby arriving at a spontaneous, total silence of the conditioned consciousness, may activate the remaining part of the consciousness. That is what they call meditation.

In meditation, the total silence of the conditioned mind opens the gate to untapped virgin part of human consciousness.[9]

The state of meditation

We might call it the state of meditation when you just are. All the roles that one takes upon oneself as the doer, the knower, the experiencer, the man, the wife... when all those roles drop away psychologically, when all the movements go into abeyance towards the known and the unknown, even towards the unknowable, then in that non-motion of your being the vibration of the Divinity, the breath of the Divinity is felt.[10]

Solitude, silence, stillness. It is a dimension for which we are not educated in the modern world. We lose balance every second minute. Meditation is a way of life in which you never lose your balance. In it an inner equipoise, an inner steadiness, an inner balance which is spontaneously there. That is the state of meditation that can be the normal dimension of the human race if it educates itself for dimensional mutation.[11]

The state of meditation is the state of unrestricted movement of the energy of Intelligence through the psychological and the sensory structure... Meditation is dehypnotizing yourself; meditation is removing the glasses of all conditioning that mind has created. Meditation is unlearning what we have learned.[12]

In the state of meditation there is no scope for any experiences or any experiencing. The state of meditation is a state of consciousness in which every mental action ceases to be. The mind is completely silent. It is not moving in any direction. The ego, the self, is in complete abeyance. He is not eliminated. You cannot eliminate the past, the memory. You cannot destroy the ego. People who have tried to kill the memory, benumb the ego, paralyze the action of the ego, mutilate their consciousness. They do not arrive at transcendence of the psyche. The mind has all the talents and capacities intact, everything is there, and yet the mind is not moving, there is a total cessation of mental activity – that is real meditation.[13]

As I understand, [meditation] is a state of consciousness in which there is no centre as the 'I' or 'me'. The consciousness through which we function usually has the centre, the 'I', the 'me' the 'self'; the subject, which divides life into the 'me' and the 'not-me', the 'I' and the 'thou', the subject and the object. The very perception of the consciousness divides life into two, the subject and the object. Such a dividing centre is not there in the state of meditation. There is only a holistic awareness, which does not divide life. No division into subject and object. The awareness of the whole permeates the being, percolates to the sense organs, to the sensual level and the sense organs, in their behaviour, manifest that non-dual consciousness, manifest that awareness of the unity of life, manifest that holistic awareness.[14]

It is only when the silence crystalises as the normal dimension of consciousness that the mutation, the quantum jump into the state of *dhyanam* occurs. It is not the result of any human effort. You cannot bring it as a result of your action. It occurs.[15]

The 'you', the 'I' cannot meditate. [Meditation] is a state of consciousness in which you can live. Once you reach there, you are there all the time. As a boy becomes a young man, there is no going back to boyhood. In the same way, when the ego is transcended there is no going back to that centre of the ego. The ego cannot rule your psyche any more. It is an instrument in the hands of a new Intelligence, but it can't rule, govern your life any more. So meditation is not something that you do. It is something that happens to you. I think it is possible to live in the dimension of meditation and yet be with people, work with people throughout your working consciousness. It is a new dimension, a new dimension [where] there is no self.[16]

Now the individualised mind feels nearly unified with the emptiness, peace and silence; all other experiences have become non-operative, nearly non-existent. So there is the individualised mind and the silence and emptiness. It feels nearly identified with it... The individualised mind used to feel unified with *vritti*, now it is unified with the space of emptiness, the space of silence... Meditation or *dhyanam* is the virgin state of the experience of emptiness and silence... the individualised mind is now really one with that experience of emptiness and peace and silence.

But still in its very subtle form, in a very purified state, the individualised mind is still there. The subtle consciousness of 'I am' or 'I am experiencing space' 'I am in the state of meditation, is still there. When that consciousness disappears there is the state of *samadhi*. It is a very subtle, harmless centre, because it is not running in the past, with the past, or running outside your body; it is harmless, but yet it is the individualised mind, it is not yet that universal mind stuff, the *drashta,* the authentic seer. There is still the thoughts, 'I am', 'I am experiencing meditation', 'I am in the state of meditation'. When that disappears, when that gets dissolved... there is the state of *samadhi*.[17]

The total relaxation of profound sleep and the dynamic awareness of meditation are very closely related to each other. Thus ... there is total relaxation and absolute freedom from I-consciousness and sex-consciousness. Meditation is being egolessly and motivelessly aware in waking hours as well as in sleep. In other words, in the state of meditation, you have the relaxation of profound sleep and awareness of waking hours. And there is a creative relationship with a new dimension of life.[18]

_____

'The state of meditation, Narada, is that state or dimension where nothing else is perceived, nothing else is known, nothing else is heard...' In the state of meditation... one does not see anything else, does not hear anything else, does not know anything else. We are getting the essence of wholeness. If meditation is a state of wholeness, the state of Brahman, what exactly happens there? Sanat Kumara says: 'You are in a state where you do not know anything, you do not see anything, you do not hear anything, you do not experience anything.' Does it not indicate then that as long as you are in a state of knowing, seeing, hearing, experiencing, you are not in the dimension of meditation?

Very poetically Sanat Kumara says that in the state of meditation you do not see anything else than yourself, you do not hear anything else than yourself. 'Than yourself' is understood – he does not say it. 'He does not think of anything else than himself, does not hear anything else than himself or herself, does not perceive anything different from himself.' He says, as long as a person sitting or living in meditation says that I know so much, he is not in a state of meditation, because knowing is information, compounded of words about an object. Knowing is an indirect contact with the help of words, but meditation has no mental operation. The mind is not moving: how is it then possible to know? [19]

_____

A person who lives in a state of meditation lives in constant creativity. He lives in innocence. He lives in the beauty of humility and pliability. That is why you find profound peace and joy around such a person. We must understand how relaxation and creativity go together. It seems to me that in the state of meditation Intelligence uses the body and the mind without any tension, conflict or contradiction. In the state of meditation the cerebral organ is extremely sensitive, sharp and ever attentive. The compass of attention is very wide and the intensity of attention is very deep because there is no centre which directs the movement, and no circumference that limits the movement.[20]

When you sit under a tree, the tree does not say there is coolness under the shade of my branches; you sit there and you feel the coolness; it relaxes the body and if you are tired you get revitalised. In the same way, if you live with or come across the persons who have this unconditional inner freedom of harmony, you feel a kind of peace. Freedom is absence of tension, conflict and contradiction. May I say freedom is unconditional relaxation, psycho-physical relaxation? Inner freedom is a dimension of consciousness; in that emptiness no movement takes place, it is a dimension in which many saints have lived in many parts of the world.

This my friends is not some poetry or theory, that is how your friend [Vimala] has lived; she discovered it and she started living in the inner freedom of emptiness, using the mind when necessary, using the verbalisation when necessary. The moment it is not warranted to use the mind, there is an inner wholeness, an inner emptiness which your friend calls the dimension of meditation.

With the authenticity of the life behind me, I can say there is a dimension of consciousness completely independent of the movement of conditionings, of the movement of thoughts, reactions. Even when the past comes up as the hangover of the past life, those reactions, thoughts, ideas, have no power over you. They cannot pollute your perception. Nothing dies inside, it only becomes non-operative; it is there; the knowledge, inheritance, memory, it is there within you, it is the substance of your neuro-chemical being, but it is non-operative, it is no longer the controller. It is there to be used when necessary, otherwise it is in a state of non-motion.[21]

It is only in the state of meditation that love can flower, that compassion can flower. You become an expression of cosmic life, as a drop of water is an expression of the ocean.[22]

The dimension of meditation, the living in meditation, is living with the awareness of the identicalness of the consciousness housed in this body and the consciousness housed in the cosmos.[23]

Meditation and concentration

Generally people call concentration meditation. They think meditation is some method, some technique, some formula, where you have to exercise the mind, you have to exercise the will, you have to make an effort... To concentrate is to focus one's attention upon a predetermined point (it can be visual or auditory – a mantra)... [Concentration, *dharana*] has nothing to do whatsoever with meditation *(dhyana)*... [Concentration] has an educational value, to strengthen the mind.[24]

Concentration is a discipline. You try to focus your attention on one point which you choose. You exclude the rest of reality and the world from the focus of your attention and you concentrate it on one point. That concentration is not meditation. The mind wants to run away to various objects and you are trying to pin it down to one point. That is what discipline is. Concentration develops the powers of the mind. It sharpens the intellect, it enriches the memory. It gives the capacity to manifest many occult powers, many hidden powers which are latent and dormant in the psyche. That is a mental activity. I feel that meditation as an all-inclusive state of awareness, an all-inclusive state of attention, is really growing into a different dimension. Meditation is a state of being.[25]

Concentration has nothing to do wjth meditation. It is the culti-
vation and development of the powers hidden in the mind.
Those who practice concentration attain... psychic powers
like clairvoyance, clairaudience, reading the thoughts of other
people. They imply the functioning of the I-consciousness on
a very subtle plane and it is not without danger to cultivate
and develop these powers.

People feel very happy when they get some visions and experiences. They feel that they are very religious, that they are
making much progress. They feel superior to others. Actually,
this is only playing around with the subconscious. There is nothing religious, leave alone spiritual, about it.[26]

You hardly come across a person who has entered a state of
meditation as a result of concentration... You may enter a
state of trance through the practice of concentration. But a
state of trance is not a state of meditation. A state of trance, a
state of having visions and extraordinary experiences indicates that there is someone to experience it. As long as there
is a possibility of an experiencer, you are nowhere near meditation. In the state of meditation there is no experiencer...
Moreover the process of concentration has a beginning and
an end in time. Whereas once the state of meditation dawns
upon you, it has no end. It is there. It is there vibrating within
you. It takes away your fragmentary existence and makes
you whole... In the state of meditation you live in that totality
like the fish lives in water. It is not permanent in the sense of
being static. It is every moment anew. It is dynamic. It seems
to me, thus, that concentration and meditation are diametri-
cally opposed to each other.[27]

Up to *dharana,* the I, the self, the me, the ego, the monitor,
whatever you call it, can assert itself, can make an effort, can
see the result of its effort in time ; it can even manipulate the
result, so it is satisfied : I have done this, I have progressed.

And naturally, through yoga *asanas, pranayama, pratya-
hara, dharana,* the dormant energies in the body, in the biological organism, in the psychological structure, which were
not tapped before, they are stimulated. The manifestation of
those activated powers is called *vibhuti* or *siddhi.* So up till
then, the enthusiasm of the I, the 'me', is tremendous, because it is doing something, it is getting something, it can
measure it, people can see what you have achieved and you
can teach it to others.[28]

Meditation is the by-product of being in the dimension of
silence. It is a mutation that occurs. But concentration, which
is a psycho-physical activity, can be practised. You can say, 'I
concentrate for two hours a day. This occult power has
developed due to concentration.' You cannot say, 'I will
meditate for two days *or* I will meditate for two hours.' You
can say, 'I will sit in silence.' A person who grows into the
dimension of meditation lives in the inner emptiness all the
twelve hours of the day.[29]

The effects of meditation

Out of meditation is born a *chitta* which has no content of
thought, emotion, feeling, which has no past, which has no
conditionings. *Chitta* which is emptiness, emptiness as a dimension of consciousness, gets born. In the beginning it lasts
for say a few hours... [and then] it slips back to into the mental or the cerebral; it becomes aware of this, again gets back
into the meditative dimension and then there is a growth into
samadhi, the dimension of invincible equipoise, invincible
peace, invincible relaxation. No action can damage the relaxation. No speaking for hours can affect the inner state of
silence and no relationships which one has to go through in
society can even touch the solitude of the consciousness.[30]

The meditative way of life transforms the individuals into human beings who have love and care, tenderness and affection, for one another. Then only can we have hope, and it is the only hope for the world, for a human society based on freedom and equality.[31]

When a person grows into this new dimension of life, it becomes possible to move through a variety of relationships without leaving any scars of memory behind. One grows into an entirely new way of living. One uses the body in a different way, and the mind is used in a qualitatively different way. Even the use of speech goes through a radical change. These changes are not brought about by a conscious effort. They take place naturally, easily and gracefully. Transformation is an event that takes place spontaneously. It can never be brought about intentionally... As soon as you determine to bring about a transformation, you become a victim of cerebral tensions.[32]

As you live at the thought level, at the level of your ideas, ideologies, or likes and dislikes, a person living in the dimension of meditation lives in inner emptiness. And when looking is necessary, the eyes look, the sight looks out of the emptiness, the inner relaxation. There is no tension. There is no exhaustion. The body may get tired, the body may get old, wrinkled, but inwardly it is always green. The greenness of life, the innocence, the humility, the tenderness of life – they are there till the last breath if the person lives in the dimension of meditation.[33]

Meditation is a state where you get a new energy, not the energy of thought, not the energy of word, not the energy of sound. Sound is an energy, thought is an energy. Thought is matter that emanates from your body, and every matter contains energy. Beyond all these energies is the energy of emptiness from which the universe has come into existence. The energy of emptiness is the energy contained in space, in silence.[34]

Meditation is the activation of the subtlemost energy of Intelligence. Meditation transports our whole being from the domination of matter, the domination of instincts and impulses, from the domination of thoughts, into the orbit of Intelligence, and the perfume of Intelligence is the energy of Awareness.[35]

Once you see that there is one basic energy permeating the whole cosmos, then the sense of otherness, of 'me' and the 'other' disappears. Not as a theory of non-duality but as a fact of life. That sense of duality, the tension of duality just drops away like the autumn leaves from the trees without causing any hurt to the mind. You do not renounce. The 'I' does not forego the sense of 'Iness', it just breaks down, gets demolished and what remains is the vibrating awareness of the oneness of that all-permeating Intelligence.[36]

Meditation as a state of being causes the total liquidation of the 'I', the centre, and brings about the activation of Supreme intelligence as a radically new energy that has no centre and no circumference; an energy born of the space of Silence which has no past and no inheritance.[37]

5. SAMADHI AND REALISATION

What is Intelligence, Love ? It cannot be described in ordinary words except to say that it can be perceived as some Energy which is all-pervading, infinite, without time. It is another dimension of consciousness which Vimalaji called 'Awareness', which cannot be known by the human mind, but it is a higher part of our being. When it is first perceived in the state of Silence, it presents itself in many experiences, which later settle in the being and become the normal abode, rather than the intense, ecstatic periods of high elevation 'as the inside adjusts to the outside'* or, Atman realises itself to be what it has always been, Paramatman. It may be felt as a Fire, as a Presence which is occupying the human being, or as a billowing Expansion. This Cosmic Consciousness, the One Unicity, which is by nature Love or Desire, has issued forth from the Absolute, whilst remaining an aspect or emanation and integral undivided Energy of that Absolute.

This eventual occurrence of a soul-infused personality is not manifested simply as some happy human being full of joy and contentment; it is something far more profound and revolutionary: it is an 'inner revolution', 'a total transformation', as Vimalaji describes it. It is true that in the personality, in the body-emotions-mind the effects of the Fire or Presence or Wholeness do become manifest. One might no-

---

* The 'inside' is the psyche, containing all the potentialities of receiving, transmitting and becoming a perfect expression and continuum of the 'outside', that is, the unlimited, infinite, fire of love, or Intelligence. The psyche, soul, atma, itself undergoes a 'refinement', of which the end result is that the individual psyche vibrates in unison with Intelligence. Then this tremendous velocity begins to be felt in the human being.

tice that the person is more interested in helping the world, that the person is more serene and relaxed, less agitated, more powerful. The person seems to be able to achieve seemingly impossible things. But most importantly, the person remains modest, one might even say, concealed, and as an act of choice, living their life as an ordinary house holder or worker in the world. The body, mind and emotions have concurrently and gradually become refined so that they are able to stand the tremendous velocity of the Fire, the Cosmic Intelligence, the Wholeness. But it is in the psyche, the soul body, the Atman, that the most profound transformation occurs. Self-realisation, Vimalaji explains, is primarily a transformation of the psyche.

Self-realisation is ultimately a development, or initiation, or unfoldment of the soul-body, the psyche, the Atma, which realises itself to be, not only a temporary individual personality but Cosmic Awareness, and in this Cosmic Awareness, views the world through its own ring-pass-not. It is in the state of Silence that the individual ego gets annihilated, not through vanishing, but through being swamped, infiltrated, usurped, engulfed in the unending endlessness of Cosmic Consciousness.

This is not an event, not an experience, not a single, defined happening, but a series of expansions of understanding, which come about through a directed, individual, determined quest, an enquiry, sadhana. Like a determined dog following the scent of its master, the psyche sniffs out the next 'step', the next moment of understanding, and, as each understanding reveals itself, it becomes apparent that it was always there, and always understood, but needed only to be recognised.

Another point which Vimalaji stressed frequently is that Rea-lisation is not something to be attained:

> Figuratively you may say he or she attained *sama-dhi* but literally, spiritually, it is a wrong statement. The person lives in meditation, the person lives in *samadhi*. He cannot attain it. It is not an artificially manipulated state of your consciousness. It is a state of living, it is a way of living.

Such a one has understood that one's true nature is nothing other than an individuated Spark of the infinite stretch of all-permeating Energy which is Love, Intelligence and Will in expression. Such a one discovers that the Cosmic Movement directs the person's life, in the sense that the movement of Divinity finds no obstruction in the bodies of the realised person. Hence much important and useful work can be achieved for upliftment of the world by such a person. Such realisation of one Being can achieve more for the world than hundreds of volunteers working to help others. This is not to dismiss the act of service in any way, rather, Vimalaji would say that to give everything utterly in pursuit of helping others is of benefit to oneself, for through dedication of the ego and voluntarily undertaken 'shocks' or difficulties which expose the human to difficulties, progress will be very rapid.

There is an even deeper dimension behind this, a total recession, in which even the movement of the Cosmic Consciousness, that Intelligence which is the projection or expression or energy of the Absolute, ceases to be. This Absolute, this Recession, of which each human constitutes an unseparated spark, cannot know Itself. It is a Void, an Abstraction, it is felt as a complete blacking-out, negation, or absence in Presence from the material world, which remains observed, but outside the Perceiver. The Void Emptiness is 'the Behind' from which emerged all this event-filled manifestation.

When the 'I' consciousness explodes it gets converted into its original pristine glory of Cosmic Consciousness. The body along with the brain becomes a container of Supreme Intelligence which is the expression of Cosmic Consciousness in the movement of relationship. This dimensional transformation is a logical consequence and a natural culmination of holistic inquiry. It is not a personal achievement. It is the privilege of anyone and everyone who has fearless readiness to live the Truth at the very moment it reveals its nature. To allow the Truth to make its abode in your consciousness and to flow freely through you neurochemical system is a great fun, accompanied by the instantaneous abolition of fear structure.[1]

In the state of samadhi, the energies contained in the physical body surrender through unconditional total relaxation and the mental energies of knowledge, thought, experience, *samskaras* are surrendered through silence. So it is the total silence of the conditional mind and total relaxation of the physical body that constitutes the essence of samadhi, the dimension of samadhi.[2]

Now do you understand the meaning of the term self-realisation? It is not the self, the petty little me, the ego that experiences something. *Atma shakshatkar*, self-realization is not an experience of the ego of something. It is not any subtle mental operation, it is not an acquisitive activity, it is a state of your whole being cleansed of all imbalances, cleansed of all impurity, vibrating with the purity of intelligence, that is self-realisation, that is meditation, that is samadhi.

When meditation becomes a normal dimension of consciousness and the energy of supreme Intelligence is released through every action, then you say that the person is living in samadhi. It is the culmination of meditation. Otherwise, people can be in the state of meditation when they are alone, living in solitude, far away from the turmoil of relationships. But at the very first touch of the interaction with people, the touch of pleasure or pain, the touch of success or failure, humiliation or honour, the state of meditation withers away and it gets replaced by the ego-centred state of misery and suffering.[3]

So samadhi is a new dimension. In that state of meditation, the sense of 'I am' is totally wiped out. Not, 'I am the body, I am the mind' —not that kind of I-am-ness— but the sense of 'I am experiencing meditation' – that last segment gets wiped out. Then there is the emptiness and silence, now the silence and space have penetrated the sense of I am and dissolved it –that is samadhi.[4]

In the state of samadhi, concentration *(dharana)* and meditation *(dhyana)* are not destroyed, but as sugar gets dissolved in water and sweetens it, in the same way, in the state of samadhi, the quality of *dharana* and *dhyana* get dissolved and enrich the samadhi. Dissolution is not destruction, dissolution is enrichment.[5]

Through the individualisation, distribution of energies into different organs, through the diversification of their functions, we were separate from the *mula prakriti* or the universal matter. In this hour of relaxation, in this hour of surrender, the separation comes to an end. As the diversification and distribution, etc. has been eliminated, you are already united with *mula prakriti* the matrix of life, the universal matter.

This is called *samadhi* which is beyond *dhyana*. *Dharana* corrects the identification. *Dhyana* through the emptiness of consciousness and relaxation of the physical body, energises, intensifies vitality. And through the elimination of the separation with the universal matter *mula prakriti* there is the dimension of samadhi. Samadhi is the cave in which the revelation will take place. It is only now a question between *mula prakriti* and *Brahman*. It is only a question between *maya* and *Ishvara*. You have already crossed from *jiva* to *mula prakriti* or *maya.*

The total relaxation of the physical and the mental results in the by-product of samadhi –a new dimension of consciousness. The transcendence from the physical and mental has already taken place. Samadhi is a supramental dimension. It is beyond thought and time. It is a purified consciousness, like the rarefied air on the mountain top. The purer the air the more rarefied it becomes. The higher you go the purer you become. It is a dimension which I have to talk about in negative terms, using terms like non-physical, non-mental, non-rational. No positive terms can be used to describe the dimension of samadhi.[6]

When your being is not divided into the observer and the observed, the seer and the seen, the doer and the act, or the experiencer and the experienced, when your being and all the faculties contained in you do not divide themselves as subject and object, then in that undivided existence of yours, in that virgin unity of your being the mystery, the secret gets revealed unto you. You cannot know it, you cannot measure it, but it gets revealed unto you. It is only when all the outgoing activities have spontaneously gone into abeyance that the revelation can occur, can happen.[7]

The word 'enlightenment' seems to be a deceptive term. It creates an idea that there is a destination called 'enlightenment' to be reached by some method or technique. In reality one has to perceive the Truth and understand it. What is called Enlightenment or Liberation may be nothing but the light of understanding or the fragrance of Truth.[8]

[Samadhi] has never appeared to me as a fixed location to be obtained. It felt rather like a river in which you were slowly submerged. When we go through the process of self-education there is a period when you are studying, when you are learning to be in Silence. After that there comes a moment when samadhi is known, at first it seems to be rather touch and go, it comes for an hour, it fades, but every times it goes on increasing in intensity and depth and if the daily lifestyle is a supportive factor then samadhi crystallizes into the ordinary dimension of consciousness.[9]

The mind feels as if it has entered the Brahman, the Divinity, the supreme Essence; as if it has fused into the cosmic... It is not a cerebral movement. It is not a chemical experience. It is not a neurological sensation. It is a tremendous happening. It is a tremendous event... As the blinking of the eyes take place effortlessly, timelessly, and the lightning flashes across the skies instantaneously, timelessly, the [Kena] Upanishad says the revelation of the Divinity or Brahman takes place in this way. [10]

A DISCUSSION ON SELF-REALISATION
WITH VIMALAJI [11]

Question: *There seem to be three major stages or dimensional shifts in the process of total transmutation, the first being when one enters Silence, the second being when the Thatness descends or occupies the being, and thirdly, the final drawing of the curtain, as Vimalaji has called it. Would this be a correct understanding, and could Vimalaji comment please?*

Vimalaji: The two stages of silence and the first experiences of 'being occupied', occur in the same dimension. But when it occupies permanently then the second dimensional shift, as you call it, takes place. There are many who cannot stand that overtaking, and they lose balance. If that 'being possessed' crystallizes at all levels, then total transformation has taken place.

Question: *When the 'state of being possessed' first occurs it seems to be almost overwhelming with a fantastic velo-city and energy, and then after a while, this sense of being swept away in the tides is replaced by a sense of bliss and communion. Would this be correct?*

Vimalaji: Yes, the first time it is felt it is overwhelming, and you have to learn to assimilate and adjust to that Energy, not remaining a foreigner to it, nor letting it be foreign to you, but letting it become a part of you, and when that sense of it being normal happens, then the dimensional change has taken place. Until then it is a transitional stage with adjustment taking place. It is a learning phase.

Question: *Is this state of actually being taken over, of be-ing used, what is called the state of* bij *samadhi, which still contains a sense that the personality is being used?*

Vimalaji: Yes, this sense of 'being possessed' which you describe, this feeling that the whole being is used by the Cosmic, belongs to the Cosmic, which moves through it, feeling that one is stepping aside to allow It to move through one, this is *bij samadhi*. When it first permeates the being there is a sense of being possessed, but gradually it becomes a natural state, so there is nothing like perceiving it as being possessed.

Question: *There seems to be a further stage in which suddenly a shift takes place, and instead of a feeling that 'Christine is being used', it becomes 'I, the Nothing, AM'. All this outside world has come upon Me, the Empty, Limitless Void. Even the Christine thing is outside Me (the Essence of the Absolute); the body-mind of the Christine thing is something I look through, but it is outside and there is nothing Inside.*

Vimalaji: It is the cosmic 'I', the cosmic 'Me', from which the whole universe proceeds. There is no sense of individuality in this 'I'. It is Infinite, unlimited.

– Would this be what is experienced when the final down flow takes place?

– It could be gradual. I don't know, but in Vimala's experience it happens in a timeless moment, a spreading, transforming, holistic event. But then again, who is to say; it could perhaps happen gradually and slowly.

Question: *Would* bij samadhi *be the state which is called the mystical marriage, which Vimalaji has referred to as the male and female energies blending? Is this Shiva and Shakti blending and is the consummation of this blending* nirbij samadhi *?*

Vimalaji: Yes, it is called the 'mystic marriage' by the Sufis and other Indian mystic sects.

Question: *When* bij samadhi *occurs, what process is taking place? Is it individual consciousness merging with universal consciousness, or is it the universal consciousness merging with the Absolute Source behind, and how does shakti relate to this process?*

Vimalaji: In *samadhi* it is not the individual and the universal consciousness getting blended together, it is not the individual retaining the universal. It is the Self understanding that It is the Self and not an Ego. The 'I' tries to resist the universal taking over, but if there is no resistance, and there is a sense of surrender and acceptance, then it comes upon you – we say 'merging'.

Question: *Which is that Energy which causes the final down-flow of Spirit; I mean, in which state does it hap-pen, in which state should the person be living? Silence, or* bij samadhi, *or does one need to be in that 'reversed' state?*

Vimalaji: When the Self understands its Cosmic Isness the universal and individual consciousnesses merge, the Individuated Self still containing something of Its own Essence, their blending is the ultimate *samadhi*. Even awareness, even assertion of universal consciousness is not there. It is sheer Isness, with nothing inside.

Question: *Is it necessary to live in the Silence for every minute of the waking hours, before the total transforma-tion can occur?*

Vimalaji: To live in the Silence is only the beginning. Once the Silence lives in you, you're moved by It because you are an expression of that Silence. You don't live in that state. It takes over your life.

Question: *Vimalaji has talked about the silken thread which is Intelligence, and that once this is built, nothing can destroy it. Would this be the antahkarana, the conscious connection which the enquirer builds whilst in the state of Silence and meditation, and where does it connect, and to what?*

Vimalaji: Earth connects you to the interplanetary Life. The Consciousnesses have their abode in that interplanetary system. The silken thread connects you to the whole inter-planetary movement. Not only are we associated with it, we are connected to it. We talk about the Consciousness which moves through the seven orbs, if required, for global purpo-ses. That relationship with the Interplanetary is there.

Question: *How do you know when it is the final mutation, that is, the down flow of spirit which will permanently fix the state and after which, Vimalaji says, one does not need to be alone, because the state is constant?*

Vimalaji: The evolution in consciousness is just a few thou-sand years old, it seems to me. A new human race with mu-tated consciousness will occur, will have to inhabit the planet in order to restore it and re-organise it according to the need of the spiritual expression of the Great Life which is the consciousness of the cosmos.

– *I was meaning in relation to total transformation of the human being.*

– Why are you so anxious about the state being fixed? You have touched the Absolute. What more can Christine want? Nothing can be permanent, no state, no level of consciousness. There is only an inexpressible, infinite potential contained in divinity. To qualify it in any way would be damaging.

My heart is no more on this earth
Nor is there a sense of belonging here.
I am far away from everywhere.
There is neither land nor sea, nor skies.
There is neither light of the sun, moon or stars
There is neither life nor death where I am.
There is neither Me nor You nor I and mine.
No words can contain that which is.
No words can translate that which is.
A relation-free Relatedness
A sound-free Eloquence.
A time-free Presence.
Is this the ultimate deathless death?
Is this the ultimate immortality?
That state in which the mind is no more,
that state which fascinates the world,
that state in which the fear of this world
and beyond disappears forever,

that state is called the Brahmi state.
The blissful, ever-creative
dimension of Turiya is ever-young,
is eternally wedded,
is ever unified with death.
That state is called the Brahmi state.
It is a spontaneous samadhi.
It is an eternal liberation beyond words.
That state is called the Brahmi state. [12]

Post Script

KATHOPANISHAD

The book, *Kathopanishad*, which was published in 2006 by Vimal Prakashan Trust, contains talks given on this Upanishad to European yoga teachers, by Vimalaji in Dalhousie in 1995.

These talks contain the essence of Vimalaji's Teaching, profound, eloquent, and spoken with great clarity from the depth of experience. Vimalaji explains that *'I am trying to share with you my understanding of the Upanishad. I had studied the Upanishads and philosophy for my Masters, at the university, and studied them with very well-known scholars of India, like Sir Sarvapalli Radhakrishnan, who was the President of India. I studied Indian Philosophy, staying with him in his house, for a few months. So I am sharing with you a non-conventional approach. If I were to talk only with the Hindus, here in India, about the Upanishads, then the interpretation would be the same but the approach would be different. Then I would try to show them how the Hindu community has imposed and grafted certain interpretations on the words of the Vedas. Here, I am sharing with you the universal content of these ancient books of wisdom, the secret principles of life.' (pp. 25-26)*

The interpretation which Vimalaji gave in her talks was very much in accord with theosophical teaching, and the Ancient Wisdom expressed in the Alice A. Bailey books, although Vimalaji had never drawn on other sources and talks, only directly from her own experience and understanding. Additionally, on various occasions, she mentioned that she also met with the Rishis who are not presently in earthly bodies. She frequently mentioned throughout her commentary on the *Kathopanishad* that her interpretation may not have been accord with the other, more traditional commentators. It is partly for this rea-son that the book is so crucially important, as it presents to us afresh the real intention of the ancient Rishis who thousands of years ago shared this knowledge. For this reason I am including in this Post Script a summary of my own understanding of the greatness of this commentary.

There is no individual personified God which sits in heaven. Human beings are responsible for their own behaviour and the Formless Essence which caused the world to manifest out of 'desire' for knowing Itself, is a neutral Principle. It is the responsibility of humans to either live in accord with this Principle, or to chose to turn away from the Reality within, their own true nature.

It could be said that the Brahman is a triplicity. *'It is a triple fire. This flame of fire, the agni, which we call the cosmos, has in it the faculty of self-knowing and self-awareness. The second aspect of the triple fire is the faculty of desire; it is the motivation force. The self-knowing, the self-awareness by themselves do not generate any movement. It is the force of desire that motivates motion in the cosmic life. And the third part of the triple flame is the movement of eternal unfolding of its own nature.' (p. 152)* These three aspects correspond to Will, Love-Wisdom, and Active Intelligence of the Alice A. Bailey books. There is the formless Void Itness or Essence from which the second fire – that of the Energy or Velocity of Mind issues forth, and is concretised in the manifestation of the myriad lives and forms of the physical world.

The human being also consists of these three fires or aspects. The human being is indeed 'condensed cosmos', containing many layers and levels of Energy and consciousness, from the gross to the formless, some visible, and some invisible, the Ultimate Reality, the Brahman, being outside time and space, and indescribable. This Ultimate Reality, this Void, this Essence, which gives issue to the world, could be said to be *Purusha*, whereas its expression, including the (to us) invisible layers of mind and psyche, are *prakriti*.

'This Parabrahman, that ultimate reality, can be indicated only by a homogeneous, self-generated sound, which is the sound of life. Wherever there is life, there this sound is the substance of that expression. Oceans or mountains or trees or birds or animals or human beings, whether they are conscious of it or not, there is a self-generated beginningless and endless sound vibrating in their being. This primal sound is the source of creation, the substance of creation, and therefore the symbol of reality' (p. 180). This is the *Om*, the 'Intelligence' as Vimalaji has called it throughout her Teaching. *'It requires a very subtle sensitivity to feel (the soundlessness of those vibrations in our life. When the noise of desire subsides, when the division caused by attractions and repulsions subsides, when the sense organs are disciplined and the mind is filled with the power of self-restraint, then... it is possible for a person to feel the sound of Om in his own body' (p. 181),* Vimalaji explains in her interpretation of *Kathopanishad*.

The difficult question of the non-existence of Atma or Soul

Perhaps the most difficult part of this Teaching is understanding the various stages and phases through which a human being passes until he or she becomes a little 'God'. 'You are That', Vimalaji frequently repeated. Yet Vimalaji made the radical statement that there is no soul, there is no Atma. What did she mean by this when many pages of *Kathopanishad* have been spent in explaining the existence of Atma (soul) in a human being?

According to Vimalaji's discussion of *Kathopanishad*, *'Lodged in your body, lodged in the cave of your heart is that ancient, eternal soundless silence. There is a communion between the silence in your conditioned consciousness and the silence as the cosmic principle in your body. There is communion between the two silences, the communion between the silence of the consciousness and silence as the eternal principle of life contained in the body, because body is the vehicle that carries the cosmic fire. Just as the ray of the sun contains the whole sun in it, in the same way, this microcosm contains the whole macrocosm in condensed form. ...This nothingness, this eternity this silence, is the nature of Atman, the reality... No-thing but silence can reach it. That Atman, that nothingness, which contains "allness" or "wholeness" was never born and never does it die'. (pp.184-85) 'The mighty power (of the unma-nifest, the unborn and therefore undying triple fire of life) in the human body is mystically described as dwelling in the crown of the head... so that mighty power is located in the head (in the brahmarandhra chakra), as it is located in the cosmos'. (pp. 412-13)*

The question is whether all this theoretical analysis is necessary. Yet Vimalaji maintained that the ancient Rishis had developed the inner exploration of the human nature as a science, that self-realisation, that perception of Energies beyond our ordinary ken, can be realised and can become part of our multi-dimensional lives. Ancient Sanskrit contained many and specific words to describe various levels of psychic and meditative awareness. Furthermore, the experience of humans who have passed through this process can be demonstrated to be an utilisation of, and growing sensitivity to, Energies as yet unperceived. The Energies undetected by science at present, will in future be shown to exist, and the way of higher evolution is open to everyone who is prepared to plunge themselves into this 'experimental science'.

Thus, the question of whether the *Atma* or soul exists is important. It is a part of the path of inner exploration to be able to understand, as well as to experience, and later to live in awareness of, our true nature which is one of ever-expanding vertical and horizontal dimensions. Indeed, the true nature of a human being is transcendental as well as immanent. Vimalaji, in her commentary differentiates between the *jivatman*, which she calls the ego, the soul (to use a Western term) and the *paramatman*.

This soul, *jivatman*, or 'higher-self', is the immanent expression in every form of that transcendental *paramatman*. 'The divinity has entered in the human body; it is immanent.' (p. 282) This 'human soul', this *jivatman* must itself undergo purification in the process of development so that all the levels and layers and dimensions of mind, emotions, and physical body can be refined, their 'vibration increased' so that eventually the human soul, consisting of these various levels of mind, can become the expression of the formless, transcendental *paramatman*. Eventually even this perfected personality or soul, having completed its divine purpose, which is to bring directly the *paramatman* into expression, will depart the individuated consciousness forever, and then only the principle of *paramatman* remains.

'In the cave of your heart is concealed the principle of immortality... those with immense patience feel the presence of that... principle of eternity, immortality, divinity, the Brahman. Atman is not an entity; it is a tattvam. It is a principle; it is energy.' (p. 522)

This then is the answer so far as we can understand it from the limited, circumscribed human condition – there is no entity, no personality, which is immortal. The personal human soul, the *jivatman*, departs after myriad incarnations, having served its purpose of revealing to the transcendental principle, its own Itness. What remains is the 'Isness of Life', which is immortal.

What is self-realisation or 'enlightenment'?

Vimalaji explained that the term enlightenment is usually employed to describe the dimensional shift which occurs in the state of silence, when all thoughts recede and the movement of 'Intelligence' that Energy of love, infinity, and eternity, is felt in the body for the first time as a powerful velocity and completely different view or perception of the world is undergone by the experiencing entity.

*'It can be felt, your body becomes like a live wire, charged
with that self-aware energy of atman... The principle of
seeing, knowing, understanding, acting, permeates the being
without becoming an entity, without becoming exclusive,
because it has its roots in cosmic life. It is united; it is not
severed or snapped away from the roots. As the ray of sun
touches the earth, that purusha has touched your heart and
manifested as your atman. Once it has entered it knows no
setting, it is there! Therefore... when that "feel" of the
presence of atman or the principle of seeing, knowing being
aware, etc. is felt, when that presence of the principle is felt,
the yogi says "This is it!" ...That's all he can say. If you ask
him to descri-be, he says, no words can describe it... It does
not crystallize into an entity. It retains its principleness of or
principlehood, the fluidity of the principle. That is why it can
permeate the whole being'. (p. 523)*

When this happens it is, in one sense, only the beginning, for
the human being now faces many life tests, in which over the
following years adjustment has to be made in the psyche, 'the
inside has to adjust to the outside', there must be a merging of
atman with *paramatman*, to that One Unicity, that movement
of Intelligence, and it must become a perpetually present Awareness.

After the revelation has taken place, there is a feeling, *'I have
seen it.' 'The revelation has taken place unto me.'* The center
of the *'me'* is at the highest level. Now the sense of separateness is at the highest level. *'I have seen it.' 'I am emancipated,' 'I am transformed,' 'I am in samadhi', 'I live in awareness.'* That identification with a feel of freedom is the subtlest
identification... the Upanishad says, he who says that I have
it knows not, and he who understands that he knows not, has
understood (pp. 535-36).

To learn to live an active life, participating, contributing to the
development of this tortured world, whilst at the same time
keeping that flame alive, keeping that voltage at a constantly
generated velocity, whilst keeping oneself available, something
happens in this state of meditation, *dhyan*, which causes the

spread blanket of endless love to become perpetually, uninter-
ruptedly a transcendental 'crystallised' dimension of cosmic
consciousness. In the Alice A. Bailey and theosophical literature this has been called the Third Initiation.

The fourth initiation, called *arhat* by the buddhists, can perhaps only be explained in the words of Vimalaji:

*When the grace of that atman or paramatman descends upon
your being in the form of revelation, you have not seen, it
has been shown unto you. It has been shown unto you, on
your own you would not have received. On your own you
have come to the point of meditation. There, all the power of
your human effort, which was gone into scientifically, step by
step, and which was bringing about qualitative transformation, that effort itself becomes irrelevant... when the third
knot is untied, the sense of separateness or even a subtle
desire to retain separateness... to have a desire for the continuity of that bliss or peace, leaves you... Then as water
enters the sponge and goes out of it, the yogi allows even this
experience of ecstasy to travel through it, without claiming it
as his own. It has happened on the orbit of human consciousness. That consciousness, dwelling in this body, has
arrived at that point, that is all...*

*When that has happened at the sensory, the psychological
and even at the mystical level, the knots are untied, then it is
immortality. The desire for separateness and exclusive ownership is mortality and awareness that one is an expression
of cosmic life is... the immortality. The consciousness may
have travelled through many bodies and if necessary cosmic
consciousness might send it back for the service of humanity
in some other body; that does not bother one. Then the revelation transports him into a divinity beyond space and time.
That communion transports the being into timelessness,
which is eternity, which is divinity, which is atman, which is
Brahman. So Nachiketa, immortality can be experienced or
communed with only in the human body; not outside it. The
form is the vessel, the nectar can be poured into it. (pp. 536-
40)*

I believe that Vimalaji could speak these words and teach us about this state because she knew it, because she travelled the long human journey, and because she arrived at that peace of dissolution, where there is no more a human personality, but only an endless expanse of a Void Everything, indescribable and unrecognisable by the small and limited human brain, a brain which nonetheless contains the mind which has the ability to bring each and every being on this earth to that same dimension of unlimited and timeless existence.

GLOSSARY

Absolute Ground of Existence : The Essence from which the phenomenal world issues forth. It cannot be known and is a mystery. It could be felt only by realised human beings as a Void, a Vacuum, a blackness full of potency, an absence of Presence and yet a Presence. No words can describe It, and the mind cannot know it.

Attachment: Psychological dependency.

Awareness *(prajna)*: Non-differentiated energy, the energy of Intelligence. The state of consciousness of one who has become enlightened or who is in the state of Silence. 'Self-awareness is not the attribute of the man-made mind, it is not a movement of the man-made mind... Awareness is the expression of cosmic life, the movement of the universal consciousness, the supramental consciousness.'

Brahman: The undercurrent of all the movement in the moving world. The vibration in every material form, without becoming contaminated, by the form, permeating everything, running through everything. The Supreme Reality which permeates the whole Cosmos.

Consciousness: 'Consciousness is an energy contained in the physical frame. Its content is thought, knowledge, memory, patterns of conditionings, reactions, experience. Self-cons-ciousness involves volition, the exercise of will, it requires *asmita,* the identification with the fixed point I. Consciousness is a human movement, voluntary, limited and partial, which can even be fragmented.'

Desire: This word is used by Vimalaji to describe the primal energy of Life. It is a pure energy emanating, contained in, an attribute of, the Absolute Itself. It accompanies Life wherever it is. It is an ingredient of Life. In the absolute ground of existence, there seems to be this primal energy of Desire which has no motivation, no direction, no destination. It is the attraction or impetus for the Brahman or Absolute to know itself. The word 'desire' becomes perverted and debased when it is misinterpreted and misdirected by the human mind which claims it and distorts it.

Dharana: The state of concentration when one focuses the mind intently and with great deliberation on one particular subject. It is a discipline of the mind.

Dharma: 'The pouring of the wholeness of your being, doing everything that you have to do with a sense of responsibility. *Dharma* is that action that joins you with the divine.'

Dhyana: The state of meditation, which is activated, or which occurs, when one has entered the state of silence. 'The state of meditation is the state of unrestricted movement of the energy of Intelligence through the psychological and the sensory structure.'

Ego: Ego is the body-mind complex which has self-consciousness, and which thinks it is an individual, acting, deciding factor, which generates thoughts and activities. It has biological and psychological needs and appears to be a separate, independent entity, but in reality this separateness is a myth, because all manifestation, including consciousness is interconnected.

Guru: 'The meeting of the disciple with the guru is one of the holiest and most sacred events that can occur in the life of a human being.' But Vimalaji pointed out that a person should not search for a guru with the conditioned brain, in order to suit a psychological requirement. The Cosmic Movement Itself would lead a person to a guru as a result of spiritual aspiration for freedom, love and truth. A psychological requirement could be for solace, for consolation, for protection, for getting temporary rest, but this is not the real purpose of a guru.

Individual: Vimalaji differentiates between 'individual' and 'individuated'. When the individual consciousness goes into non-action, that is, refuses to become involved in the stream of human thought and conditioning, then there is awareness, as distinct from self-consciousness. But consciousness remains because it cannot be destroyed. Thus the individual is functioning in several dimensions of consciousness, awareness, and meditation.

'Individuality is the manifestation of the non-differentiated totality. There is particularity on the physical level and there is manifestation of the collective human consciousness on the psychological level. There is no individuality on the mental plane. Merging into oneness, means that the personality merges, vanishes, and particularity melts away. Such a person becomes "a condensed expression of the totality" The individuated Energy of the Wholeness persists after death.'

Inner Revolution: 'Self-realisation, enlightenment, is an "holistic revolution in the psyche" which occurs in the state of *dhyanam* (meditation). *Atma shakshatkar*, self-realization, is not an experience of the ego of something. It is not any subtle mental operation, it is not an acquisitive activity, it is a state of your whole being cleansed of all imbalances, cleansed of all impurity, vibrating with the purity of intelligence; that is self-realisation, that is meditation, that is Samadhi.'

Intelligence: 'This is the movement of the universal consciousness, the cosmic consciousness. When that universal Intelligence moves in a human being, it is called Awareness, which is the effect of that movement. This movement of Intelligence is an expression of the Absolute. It is pure seeing energy *(chiti shakti)*, untouched by human mind or thought. It is a subtle Energy born of the emptiness of Silence.'

Inquirer *(sadhaka)*: A person who searches for divinity, for the inner Reality, for Truth, through 'self-education', through the science of the exploration and investigation of consciousness, which begins by means of the mind as an instrument through which higher or finer states of consciousness, or awareness, will be revealed.

Isness (existential Essence) : When the 'inside merges with the outside', when Atma or individuated awareness merges with Paramatma, or universal cosmic consciousness, then the state of Isness, or Thatness, is realised. Called Isness because there is no past and no future but merely a completed perfection, Wholeness, a feeling of triumph, of completion, of abstraction.

Karma: Karma is derived from the root 'to do', 'to act'. One meaning is, that which is acted upon, that which is done. Karma is also 'figuratively used to denote your inheritance, your physical structure, your psychological conditioning. As a human being it is your karma to be born in a conditioned human frame.'

Kundalini: Sometimes referred to as 'the serpent power', it is a physical, but invisible energy contained in the *prana,* which becomes stimulated through the practice of silence. It then rises from the base of the spine, passing through and enlivening the chakras, (vortex of prana), so that each chakra's individual mysterious and potent power becomes manifest.

Maya: 'What is called maya is the diversity that you see sensually in the manifest world around you. Maya is a code-word to indicate that which is only relatively real, that is to say, that which is ever-changing.'

Meditation, state of : see *dhyana*.

Mutation: Mutation is a dimensional transformation. The inner mutation is the dimensional shift which occurs in the state of silence, when an individual becomes aware that there is no individual personal ego, but only the one infinite, all-permeating, all-loving, Unicity. The blending of the individual consciousness and the cosmic consciousness has occurred. 'From the dimension of the "I", the "self", there is a quantum jump into the Allness or Isness'.

Observation: Observation could be called a first step in the process of 'self-education' *(sadhana)* or enquiry; it is one means by which a person can understand the nature of the human ego. By observing thoughts, when one sits quietly alone, one learns to stop the thoughts from entering the mind. It is a state of 'reaction-free attentiveness'. This is practiced at the level of the mind and therefore involves effort. When the individual consciousness enters the state of silence, which is beyond the mind, effort is no longer needed. Then one is in a state of 'relaxation'.

Prana: The invisible, vital energy, the vital breath system, the invisible energy or 'fire' which is a constituent or emanation of the Brahman, and which activates and underlies and is interwoven with the human biological system.

Psyche: Vimalaji uses this word to describe the soul, when it associates itself with the mind, and considers that transformation in the psyche results in realisation. It is seen as part of *prakriti,* or matter, a field of expression of the Monad or Absolute, whereas the Purusha is the Absolute Ground of Existence, the Father aspect, or Spirit.

Raja Yoga: A holistic path, which is the culmination of the combination of the various branches of yoga. Its teaching takes into account the whole of life, meaning that the individual should purify the physical, the emotional, the mental body whilst simultaneously trying to understand the truth of one's inner being.

Relaxation: This is a code word which sounds generalized and abstract, but in fact has a specific meaning. When in the state of silence, which may be entered after the mind has learnt how to become empty of thoughts (which involves effort), there is effortlessness, there is no longer the struggle to watch, to direct, to exclude. Relaxation is non-effort, lack of any tension, no effort of trying, in which Intelligence comes into play.

Rishi: The word Rishi is derived from a Sanskrit root which implies 'to perceive'. The word 'sage' does not explain the nuances contained in the word 'Rishi' Vimalaji has explained. Rishi means a person of purified perception, austerity to live the perception as it has taken place and the capacity to teach if students come to them.

Sadhaka: One who practices *sadhana* (spiritual discipline).
see 'Inquirer'

Sadhana: Spiritual discipline (Vimalaji would also say 'enquiry' or 'self-education).

Samadhi : There are various levels and degrees of Samadhi which have been technically described in Patanjali's *Yoga Sutras* and other Sanskrit Teachings. *Samadhi*, according to Vimalaji's Teaching, occurs in the state of *dhyanam* (meditation), as *bij samadhi* (samadhi with the 'seed' of being the consciousness occupying two dimensions). It could be said that there are several 'degrees' or 'dimensional shifts' which occur.

In the state of Silence the Energy of the One Unicity, the Wholeness, Intelligence, is felt. When this energy of Love is felt pouring down in all levels and layers of the being, including the physical body, it is called *bij samadhi*.

Nirbij samadhi, samadhi without seed, is that state of aware-ness where there is a complete dissolution of the individual in the Brahman or Absolute. In Theosophy it is called 'monadic consciousness'. The Brahman or Absolute within every human is changeless.

Self-Awareness: When the Self is finally aware of Itself as Itself in all Its glory. Self-Realisation. It could be said that the-re are four 'stages' in the process of self-realisation:

> 1) Observation of thoughts which eventually results in
>
> 2) The state of Silence in which
>
> 3) The Wholeness is felt in the individual being *(bij sa-madhi)*,
>
> 4) The individual becomes merged with the Whole-ness, perceives itself as the Wholeness viewing itself through a person's psyche, Behind this Universal, Cosmic Consciousness is a Void, an Absolute Abst-raction, which is sometimes called *nirbij samadhi and* which cannot be known.

Self-Consciousness: Same meaning as consciousness (see above).

Silence: 'Reaction-free perceptivity', another dimension of consciousness in which the world is perceived through the pure seer, either individuated or extended. When there is that reaction-free, non-evaluatory perception, or attentiveness, then the silence as a dimension of consciousness gets activated. 'Then silence comes to life, the movement of thought goes into abeyance, and with the movement of thought the move-ment of time as we know it also comes to a standstill. Then there is that total relaxation of the movement of thought; total relaxation of the so-called "me" or "ego"; total relaxation of the known energies, the conditioned energies, and one is in the marvelous space of silence'. Silence, then, is not an experience of the conditioned mind.

Space inside: In the state of Silence the sense of being an ego, with that tainted, self-interested feeling of viewing the world from the personal egotistical dimension, is deactivated. When the ego is dissolved, then in the dimension of Silence there is the awareness of emptiness or 'space inside'. Concurrently with this, the 'movement of Intelligence' or the perception on all levels and layers of being of an Energy which is Love, and which pours down into the being, is felt.

Total Transformation: Same meaning as 'inner revolution'.

Wholeness: It is experienced in the state of meditation, which occurs in the state of Silence. Wholeness is signaled to the being by a vibration. The being in the state of silence perceives the vibration and all the qualities which accompany it are also known automatically in the awareness of Wholeness—namely, infinity, eternity, all-pervasiveness, Love, Fire.

Yoga: The consummation of human growth, which is union with the Divinity.

REFERENCES

Vimala thakar: A Life Sketch

[1] Thakar, Vimala (1971): *Totality in Essence,* Delhi: Motilal Banarasidass, p.105.

[2] Townend, Christine (2002): *The Hidden Master,* Delhi: Motilal Banarsidass.

[3] Thakar, Vimala (1989): *On an Eternal Voyage,* Ahmedabad: Vimal Prakashan Trust, pp. 67-68.

[4] — (1991): *Glimpses of Ishavasya,* Ahmedabad: Vimal Prakashan Trust, p.138.

[5] — (1971): *Totality in Essence,* Delhi: Motilal Banarsidass, p.11.

[6] *Kena Upanishad,* p. 315.

[7] Thakar, Vimala (1989): *On an Eternal Voyage,* Ahmedabad: Vimal Prakashan Trust, p. 28.

[8] Ibid.: 46.

[9] Personal communication, Dalhousie, 2000.

[10] Ibid.

[11] *Friendly Communion,* p. 22.

[12] Thakar, Vimala (2001) : "The Beauty of Nothingness", in : *Friendly Communion,* Ahmedabad: Vimal Prakashan Trust, p. 34.

PART ONE
MAN AND THE UNIVERSE

1. Macrocosm and Microcosm

[1] *Path to Nirvana,* p.19.

[2] Ibid.:18.

[3] Thakar, Vimala (1998): *Yoga beyond Meditation,* Vimalaji's Dialogues on "Yoga Sastras", Ahmedabad: Vimal Prakashan Trust, p.78.

[4] *Being and Becoming,* 1989, p.1.

[5] *A Scientific Outlook on the Integration through Education,* pp. 9-12

[6] *The Invincible,* Vol. XI n° 4, Ahmedabad: Vimal Prakashan Trust, October-December 1995: 6-7.

[7] *Vimalaji and her Perspective of Life,* 1998, pp.17-18.

[8] *The Invincible,* Vol.V n° 2, Summer, Ahmedabad: Vimal Prakashan Trust, 1988: 24.

[9] Thakar, Vimala (1990) : *The Message of Chandogya,* Part II. Ahmedabad: Vimal Prakashan Trust, p. 262.

[10] *The Invincible,* Vol. VIII n° 2, Ahmedabad: Vimal Prakashan Trust, April-June, 1991: 13.

[11] *Vimalaji and her Perspective of Life,* 1998, p. 4.

[12] Ibid.: 29-30.

[13] *The Invincible,* Vol. IX n° 2, Ahmedabad: Vimal Prakashan Trust, April-June, 1992: 9.

[14] *The Invincible,* Vol. IX n° 3, Ahmedabad: Vimal Prakashan Trust, July-September.

[15] *The Invincible,* Vol. VII n° 2, Ahmedabad: Vimal Prakashan Trust, April-June, 1990: 23.

[16] *Being and Becoming,* p. 3.

[17] Ibid.:10.

[18] Ibid.:15-16.

[19] *Meditation in Daily Life,* 1998.

[20] *The Art of Dying while Living,* p.102.

[21] *A Scientific Outlook on the Integration through Education,* pp. 9-12.

[22] *Vimalaji and her Perspective of Life,* 1998, p.12.

[23] Ibid.: 17-18.

[24] Thakar, Vimala (1989):*Glimpses of Raja Yoga,* Ahmedabad: Vimal Prakashan Trust, p.16.

[25] *The Invincible,* Vol. XI n° 2, Ahmedabad: Vimal Prakashan Trust, April-June, 1995: 19-20.

[26] *Vimalaji and her Perspective of Life,* 1998, p. 3.

2. Love and Desire

[1] *Himalayan Pearls,* 1989, p. 112.

[2] *The Eloquence of Living,* p. 44.

[3] *The Invincible,* Vol. IX n°1, Ahmedabad: Vimal Prakashan Trust, January-March, 1992 : 20.

[4] *Silence in action,* p. 44.

[5] *The Invincible,* Vol. V n° 2, Ahmedabad: Vimal Prakashan Trust, Summer, 1988 :18-19.

[6] *Ego,* Emergence and merging back of the I-process, 1993, p. 68

[7] *The Invincible,* Vol. VI n° 3, Ahmedabad: Vimal Prakashan Trust, July-September, 1989 :4.

[8] Thakar, Vimala (1996): *Yoga beyond Meditation,* Vimalaji's Dialogues on "Yoga Sastras", Dalhousie, Ahmadabad, Vimal Prakashan Trust, p. 93.

[9] *A Scientific Outlook on the Integration through Education,* pp. 12-13

[10] *Himalayan Pearls,* 1989, p. 59.

[11] Ibid.: 62-63.

[12] Ibid.: 61.

[13] *The Invincible,* Vol. VIII n° 2, Ahmedabad: Vimal Prakashan Trust, April-June, 1991 :14-15.

[14] Thakar, Vimala (1991): *The Message of Chandogya,* Part II, Ahmedabad: Vimal Prakashan Trust, pp. 332-33.

[15] *Living a truly religious life,* p. 74.

[16] Thakar, Vimala (1991): *The Message of Chandogya*, Part II, Ahmedabad: Vimal Prakashan Trust, pp. 336-37.

[17] *Himalayan Pearls*, 1989, p.134.

[18] *Path to Nirvana*, p.19.

3. Mind and Ego

[1] Thakar, Vimala (1991): *Glimpses of Raja Yoga*, Ahmedabad: Vimal Prakashan Trust, p. 93.

[2] Ibid.: 95.

[3] Ibid.: 42.

[4] Ibid.: 88.

[5] *Kena Upanishad*, p.189.

[6] *The Invincible*, Vol. VI n° 3, Ahmedabad: Vimal Prakashan Trust, July-September, 1989: 1-4.

[7] *The Invincible*, Vol. IX n° 3, Ahmedabad: Vimal Prakashan Trust, July-September 1993.

[8] *Towards Total Transformation*, Berkeley, 1970, pp.18-19.

[9] *The Invincible*, Vol. IX n° 4, Ahmedabad: Vimal prakashan Trust, October-December, 1993: 6.

[10] Thakar, Vimala (1971): *Totality in Essence*, Delhi: Motilal Banarasidass, p. 69.

[11] *The Invincible*, Vol. IV n° 4, Ahmedabad: Vimal Prakashan Trust, July-August, 1987 :15.

[12] Ibid.:14-15.

[13] *Through Silence to Meditation*, 1998: 26-27.

[14] Thakar, Vimala (1991): *The Message of Chandogya*, Part II, Ahmedabad: Vimal Prakashan Trust, p. 279.

[15] *Path to Nirvana*, p. 9.

[16] *Ego, Emergence and merging back of the I-process*, 1993, p. 39.

[17] Ibid.: 22.

[18] *The Invincible*, Vol. IX n° 2, Ahmedabad: Vimal Prakashan Trust, April-June: 1993.

[19] *Ego, Emergence and merging back of the I-process*, 1993; pp.132-33.

[20] *Personal Discovery of Truth*, 1999, pp. 18-19.

[21] *The Invincible*, 1988, Vol. V n° 3, Ahmadabad: Vimal Prakashan Trust, 1988 : 24.

[22] *What is meditation ?* p. 60.

[23] *The Invincible*, Vol. IX n° 2, Ahmedabad: Vimal Prakashan Trust, April-June, 1992 : 9.

4. Human Life

[1] Thakar, Vimala (1971): *Totality in Essence*, Delhi: Motilal Banarasidass, p. 11

[2] Thakar, Vimala (1991): *Glimpses of Raja Yoga,* Ahmedabad: Vimala Prakashan Trust, pp. 28-29.

[3] *The Art of Dying while Living,* 1996, p. 4.

[4] Ibid.: 68.

[4a] Ibid.: 3.

[5] *Radical Peace,* Holland, 1990, p. 8.

[6] Ibid.: 9.

[7] Ibid.: 22.

[8] *The Invincible,* Vol. XVI n° 1, Ahmedabad: Vimal Prakashan Trust, January-June, 2000: 19.

[9] Thakar, Vimala (1991): *Glimpses of Raja Yoga,* Ahmedabad: Vimala Prakashan Trust, p. 113.

[10] *Personal Discovery of Truth,* 1999, p. 58.

[11] *The Art of Dying while Living,* 1996, p. 102.

[12] *Personal Discovery of Truth,* 1999, p. 46.

[13] *New Year Message,* November I[st], 2000, pp. 4-5.

[14] *Ego,* Emergence and merging back of the I-process, 1993, p. 33.

[15] *The Invincible,* Vol. XI n° 2, Ahmedabad: Vimal prakashan Trust, April-June, 1995: 19-20.

[16] Ibid.: 11-12.

[17] Ibid.: 11-12.

[18] *The Invincible,* Vol. IV n° 2, Vimal Prakashan Trust, March-April, 1987: 118.

[19] *Silence in action,* p. 44.

[20] Thakar, Vimala (1971): *Totality in Essence,* Delhi: Motilal Banarasidass, p.100

[21] *The Invincible,* Vol. IV n° 4, Vimal Prakashan Trust, July-August, 1987: 15.

[22] Thakar, Vimala (1971): *Totality in Essence,* Delhi: Motilal Banarasidass, p. 8.

[23] *Towards Total Transformation,* Berkeley, 1970, p. 56.

[24] Thakar, Vimala (1971): *Totality in Essence,* Delhi: Motilal Banarasidass, p.12.

[25] Ibid.:107.

[26] *The Invincible,* Vol. X n°1, Ahmadabad: Vimal Prakashan Trust, January-March: 1993.

[27] *Why Meditation?* p. 57.

[28] *Towards Total Transformation,* Berkeley, 1970, p. 46.

[29] *The Invincible,* Vol. X n°4, Ahmedabad: Vimal Prakashan Trust, 1993: 1-3.

[30] *The Invincible,* Vol. V n° 3, Ahmedabad: Vimal Prakashan Trust, 1988: 9.

[31] *The Invincible,* Vol. X n° 3, Ahmedabad: Vimal Prakashan Trust, July-September, 1994: 8-9.

[32] *The Invincible,* Vol. XV n°1, Ahmedabad: Vimal Prakashan Trust, January-June, 1999.

[33] *The Invincible*, Vol. X n°1, Vimal Prakashan Trust, January-March, 1993.

5. Spirituality - Yoga

[1] *Through Silence to Meditation*, p. 44.

[2] *The Invincible*, Vol. V n° 1, Spring, Ahmedabad: Vimal Prakashan Trust, 1988: 23.

[3] *Science and Spirituality*, 1988, pp. 37-38.

[4] *The Invincible*, Vol. XI n° 3, Ahmedabad: Vimal Prakashan Trust, July-September, 1995: 1-3.

[5] *The Invincible*, 1988, Vol. V n° 2, Summer, Ahmedabad: Vimal prakashan Trust, p. 22

[6] Thakar, Vimala (1971): *Totality in Essence*, Delhi: Motilal Banarasidass, p. 24.

[7] Ibid.: p.75.

[8] *Meditation in Daily Life*, p.10.

[9] *New Year Message*, November 1st, 2000, pp. 1-3.

[10] Thakar, Vimala (1991): *Glimpses of Raja Yoga*, Vimala Prakashan Trust, p.139.

[11] *The Invincible*, Vol. IX n° 2, Ahmedabad: Vimal Prakashan Trust, April-June, 1992 :11.

[12] *The Invincible*, Vol. IV n° 5, Ahmedabad: Vimal Prakashan Trust, September-October, 1987: 3.

[13] *The Art of Dying While Living*, p.116.

[14] *The Invincible*, Vol. VII n° 2, Ahmedabad: Vimal Prakashan Trust, April-June, 1990 : 8-9.

[15] *The Invincible*, Vol. VIII n° 2, Ahmedabad: Vimal Prakashan Trust, April-June, 1991:11-12.

[16] *Life is to be related*, pp. 41-42.

[17] "Based on three talks on the Bhagavad Gita" in: *The Invincible*, Vol. IX, n° 2, 3, 4, 1993.

[18] *The Invincible*, Vol. IX n° 3, Ahmedabad: Vimal Prakashan Trust, July-September, 1992.

[19] *Living a Truly Religious Life*, 1998, p. 84.

[20] *Towards Total Transformation*, Berkeley, 1970, p. 56.

[21] Thakar Vimala (1991): *The Message of Chandogya*, Part II, Ahmedabad: Vimal Prakashan Trust, p. 331.

[22] Thakar, Vimala (1991): *Glimpses of Raja Yoga*, Ahmedabad: Vimala Prakashan Trust, pp. 30-31.

[23] *Ego*, Emergence and merging back of the I-process, 1993, p. 30.

[24] Townend, Christine (2002): *The Hidden Master*, Delhi: Motilal Banarsidass.

[25] *Ego*, Emergence and merging back of the I-process, 1993, pp. 23-26.

[26] *The Invincible*, Vol. V n° 2, Ahmedabad: Vimal Prakashan Trust, Summer, 1998: 22.

[27] Thakar, Vimala (1991): *The Message of Chandogya Part II*, Ahmedabad: Vimal Prakashan Trust, pp. 233-34.

[28] —(1991): *Glimpses of Raja Yoga*, Ahmedabad: Vimala Prakashan Trust, p. 4.

[29] —(1991): *The Message of Chandogya*, Part II, Ahmedabad: Vimal Prakashan Trust, p. 228.

[30] *Himalayan Pearls*, 1989, p. 139.

[31] *Glimpses of Ishavasya*, pp. 144–151.

[32] *The Invincible*, Vol. VI n° 3, Ahmedabad: Vimal Prakashan Trust, July-September, 1989, pp.1-4

[33] *The Invincible*, Vol. VII n° 2, Ahmedabad: Vimal Prakashan Trust, April-June, 1990: 8-9.

[34] Thakar, Vimala (1971): *Totality in Essence*, Delhi: Motilal Banarasidass, pp. 39-40.

[35] Townend, Christine (2005): *Insights into the Bhagavad Gita*, Delhi: Motilal Banarsidass, p. 105.

[36] Thakar, Vimala (1971): *Totality in Essence*, Delhi: Motilal Banarsidass, p. 43.

[37] "Parish, Chris, Set them on Fire! Portrait of a modern sage", in :*What is Enlightenment* , Fall/Winter 2001: 222.

[38] Message on the occasion of Vimalaji's birthday, Mont Abu, April 1992.

[39] *The Invincible*, Vol. XVI n° 2, Ahmedabad: Vimal Prakashan Trust, July-December, 2000: 7.

[40] *The Invincible*, Vol. XVI n° 1, Ahmedabad: Vimal Prakashan Trust, January-June, 2000: 14.

[41] *Himalayan Pearls*, 1989, pp.133-136.

[42] "Based on three talks on the Bhagavad Gita", in: *The Invincible*, Vol. IX, n° 2-4, 1993.

[43] *The Invincible*, Vol. IX n° 4, Ahmedabad: Vimal Prakashan Trust, October-December, 1993: p.6

[44] Based on three talks on the Bhagavad Gita, in: *The Invincible*, Vol. IX, n° 2-4,1993.

[45] Ibid.

[46] Thakar, Vimala (2005): *Insights into the Bhagavad Gita*, Delhi : Motilal Banarsidass, pp. 52-53.

[47] —(1991): *Glimpses of Raja Yoga*, Ahmedabad: Vimala Prakashan Trust, p.16.

[48] "Based on three talks on the Bhagavad Gita", in: *The Invincible*, Vol. IX, n° 2-4, 1993.

[49] Thakar, Vimala (1991): *The Message of Chandogya*, Part II, Ahmedabad: Vimal Prakashan Trust, p. 373.

50 Ibid.: 376-77.
51 Ibid.: 149.
52 Ibid.: 149-50.

PART TWO:
THE INNER REVOLUTION
1. Introduction
1 *Comments on Kena Upanishad*, p. 282.
2 Thakar, Vimala (1998): *Yoga beyond Meditation*, Vimalaji's Dialogues on "Yoga Sastras", Ahmedabad: Vimal Prakashan Trust, p. 95.
3 *The Invincible*, Vol. II n°1, Ahmedabad: Vimal Prakashan Trust, January-February, 1985: 3-4.
4 Thakar, Vimala (1998): *Yoga beyond Meditation*, Vimalaji's Dialogues on "Yoga Sastras", Ahmedabad: Vimal Prakashan Trust, p.100.
5 Ibid.:101-102.
6 *Comments on Kena Upanishad*, p. 242.
7 *Personal Discovery of Truth*, 1999, pp. 44-46.
8 *The Invincible*, Vol. IV n° 5, Ahmedabad: Vimal Prakashan Trust, September-October, 1987:19.

2. Self-Observation
1 *The Invincible*, Vol. IV n° 2, Ahmedabad: Vimal Prakashan Trust, March-April, 1987: 21.
2 *Personal Discovery of Truth*, 1999, p. 16.
3 *The Invincible*, Vol. II n° 1, Ahmedabad: Vimal Prakashan Trust, January-Febuary, 1985: 20.
4 *The Invincible*, Vol. XVI n° 2, Ahmedabad: Vimal Prakashan Trust, July-December, 2000: 12-15.
5 Thakar, Vimala (1998):*Through Silence to Meditation*, Ahmedabad: Vimal Prakashan Trust, pp.18-21.
6 *Life is to be related*, 1982: 9-10.
7 Thakar, Vimala (1998): *Through Silence to Meditation*, Ahmedabad: Vimal Prakashan Trust, pp. 22-25.
8 *The Invincible*, Vol. X n°1, Ahmedabad: Vimal Prakashan Trust, January-March, 1994: 31.
9 *Towards Total Transformation*, Berkeley, 1970, pp. 81-82.
10 Thakar, Vimala (1998): *Through Silence to Meditation*, Ahmedabad: Vimala Prakashan Trust, pp. 25-26.
11 *Personal Discovery of Truth*, 1999, pp.18-19.
12 *Life is to be related*, 1982, pp. 10-11.
13 Ibid.: 48.
14 *Meditation in Daily Life*, 1998, pp. 17-18
15 *The Invincible*, Vol. XI n° 3, Ahmedabad: Vimal Prakashan Trust, July-September, 1995: 7.

3. The Dimension of Silence

1 *Silence in Action,* pp. 21-22
2 *Towards Total Transformation,* Berkeley, 1970, p. 81.
3 *The Invincible,* Vol. XV n°1, Ahmedabad: Vimal Prakashan Trust, January-June, 1999:23.
4 *Thakar, Vimala (1998): Through Silence to Meditation,* Ahmedabad: Vimal Prakashan Trust, p.13.
5 *What is Meditation?* pp.19-20.
6 *Meditation in Daily Life,* 1998, p.21.
7 *The Invincible,* Vol. II n°1, Ahmedabad: Vimal Prakashan Trust, January-February, 1985: 20.
8 *Meditation in Daily Life,* 1998, pp.18-19.
9 *The Invincible,* Vol. XVI n° 2, Ahmedabad: Vimal Prakashan Trust, July-December, 2000: 14.
10 *Living a truly religious Life,* 1996, pp. 55-56.
11 *The Invincible,* Vol. II n°1, Ahmedabad: Vimal Prakashan Trust, January-Febuary, 1985: 20.
12 *Living a truly religious Life,* 1996, p. 56.
13 *Silence in action,* p. 22.
14 *What is Meditation?* p. 24.
15 *The Invincible,* Vol. X n° 2, Ahemadabad: Vimal Prakashan Trust, April-June, 1991: 24-28.
16 *Personal Discovery of Truth,* 1999, p. 31.
17 *What is Meditation?* pp. 25-26.
18 Ibid.: 20-21.
19 *The Invincible,* Vol. X n° 2, Ahmedabad: Vimal Prakashan Trust, April-June, 1991: 24-28.
20 *Meditation in Daily Life,* p. 22.

4. Meditation

1 *What is Meditation?* pp. 1-2.
2 *Why Meditation?* 1974, p. 51.
3 Thakar, Vimala (1998): *Through Silence to Meditation,* Ahmedabad: Vimala Prakashan Trust, p.13.
4 *The Invincible,* Vol. VI n°3, Ahemadabad: Vimal Prakashan Trust, July-September, 1989: 22.
5 Thakar, Vimala (1991): *Glimpses of Raja Yoga,* Ahmedabad: Vimala Prakashan Trust, pp. 89-91.
6 *What is Meditation?* pp. 37-38.
7 *Silence in action,* p. 54.
8 *The Invincible,* Vol. V n° 2, Ahmedabad: Vimal Prakashan Trust, Summer, 1988: 16-18.
9 *Silence in Action,* pp. 66-67.
10 *The Invincible,* Vol. V n° 2, Ahmedabad: Vimal Prakashan Trust, Summer, 1988: 16-18.

[11] *What is Meditation ?* p. 22.

[12] Thakar, Vimala (1991): *Message of Chandogya,* Part II, pp.295-96.

[13] *Towards Total Transformation,* Berkeley, 1970, pp. 63-64.

[14] *What is Meditation?* pp. 2-3.

[15] *The Invincible,* Vol. XVI n° 2, Ahemadabad, Vimal Prakashan Trust, July-December, 2000: 15.

[16] *The Invincible,* Vol. IV n° 2, Ahmedabad: Vimal Prakashan Trust, March-April, 1987: 19.

[17] Thakar, Vimala (1998): *Yoga beyond Meditation ,* Vimalaji's Dialogues on "Yoga Sastras", Ahmedabad: Vimal Prakashan Trust, p.184-88.

[18] *Meditation,* Book Two, pp. 11-12.

[19] Thakar, Vimala (1991): *Message of Chandogya,* Part II, Ahmedabad: Vimal Prakashan Trust, pp. 264-66

[20] *Meditation,* Book Two, pp. 13-16

[21] *The Invincible,* Vol.X n°1, Ahmedabad: Vimal Prakashan Trust, January-March, 1994 : 34-35.

[22] *Life as Teacher,* 1991, pp.159-160.

[23] *What is meditation?* p. 28.

[24] *Why Meditation?* 1974, p. 52.

[25] *Towards Total Transformation,* Berkeley, 1970, pp. 76-77.

[26] Thakar, Vimala (1991): *Message of Chandogya,* Part II, Ahmedabad: Vimal Prakashan Trust, pp. 284-85.

[27] *Silence in action,* pp. 53-56.

[28] Thakar, Vimala (1971): *Totality in Essence,* Delhi: Motilal Banarsidass, p. 72.

[29] *What is Meditation?* pp. 33-34

[30] *The Invincible,* Vol. XVI n° 2, Ahmedabad: Vimal Prakashan Trust, July-December, 2000 : 11-15.

[31] *Silence in action,* p. 44.

[32] *Meditation,* Book Two, pp.16-18.

[33] *The Invincible,* Vol. XVI n° 2, Ahmedabad: Vimal Prakashan Trust, July-December, 2000: 11-15.

[34] *What is Meditation?* pp. 24-25.

[35] Thakar, Vimala (1991): *Glimpses of Raja Yoga,* p. 91.

[36] *The Invincible,* Vol. VI n° 3, Ahmedabad: Vimal Prakashan Trust, July-September, 1989:1-4.

[37] *The Invincible,* Vol. IX, n° 2, Ahmedabad: Vimal Prakashan Trust, 1992: 9.

5. Samadhi and Realisation

[1] *The Invincible,* Vol. IX n° 2, Ahmedabad: Vimal Prakashan Trust, April-June, 1992 : 9

[2] "Based on three talks on the Bhagavad Gita", in : *The Invincible,* Vol. IX, n° 2-4, 1993.

[3] Thakar, Vimala (2005): *Insights into the Bhagavad Gita,* Delhi: Motilal Banarsidass, pp. 32-33.

[4] Thakar, Vimala (1998): *Yoga beyond Meditation,* Vimalaji's Dialogues on "Yoga Sastras", Ahmedabad: Vimal Prakashan Trust, P. 187.

[5] Ibid.: 92-193.

[6] *The Invincible,* Vol. IX n° 2, Ahmedabad: Vimal Prakashan Trust, 1993

[7] *The Invincible,* Vol. X n° 4, Ahmedabad: Vimal Prakashan Trust, October-December, 1994: 3.

[8] *The Invincible,* Vol. XIV n°2, Ahmedabad: Vimal Prakashan Trust, July-December, 1998: 20.

[9] Townend, Christine (2002): *The Hidden Master,* Delhi: Motilal Banarsidass.

[10] *Kena Upanishad,* pp. 211-13.

[11] Townend, Christine (2002):*The Hidden Master,* Delhi: Motilal Banarsidass, New Delhi, 2002.

[12] *The Invincible,* Vol. XII n° 2, Ahmedabad: Vimal Prakashan Trust, July-December, 1996: 24.

BOOKS ON VIMALA THAKAR*

The Art of dying while living

Benares University talks, 1970

Being and becoming

The Benediction of being alive

Beyond Awareness, 1974

Blossoms of Friendship

A Challenge to Youth, 1974

Ego- Emergence and merging back of the I-process, 1993

Eloquence of Action

Eloquence of Living

Eloquent Ecstasy, 1962

Exploring Freedom

Fear not Life

The Flame of Life, 1962

Friendly Communion (poems), 1961-2000

From Heart to Heart, 1965

From Intellect to Intelligence

Glimpses of Ishavasya

Glimpses of Kena, 1994

---

* Unless otherwise stated, the following books, which have provided material for this book, have been published by Vimal Prakashan Trust, Ratman Tower, Flat No. 103, B/H Chief Justice Bungalow, Judges Bungalow Road, Bokadev, Ahmedabad-54, India

Glimpses of Raja Yoga, 1989

Himalayan Pearls, 1988

Insights into the Bhagavad Gita, Delhi,
Motilal Banarsidass, 2005

Life and Living

Life as Teacher, 1991

Life as Yoga

Life is Movement

Life is to be related, 1987

Living a truly religious life, 1995

Meditation- a way of life, 1998

Meditation books (1-4)

The Meditative way, 1968

The Message of Chandogya, Part one, 1990

The Message of Chandogya, Part two

Mutation of Mind

The Mystery of Silence, 1976

On an eternal Voyage, 1989

Passion for Life

The Path of Nirvana, 1995

Personal Discovery of Truth, 1999

Pilgrimage within

Radical Peace

Science and Spirituality, 1986

Scientific Outlook on the Integration through Education

Silence in Action, 1986

Spirituality and social action

Talks in Australia, 1977

Through silence to meditation, 1987

Totality in Essence, Delhi, Motilal Banarsidass, 1971

Towards Total Transformation, Berkerley, 1970

Urgency of self-discovery

Vimalaji and her perspective of life, 1994

Vimalaji on intensive self-education, 1987

Vimalaji on national problems

Voyage into oneself, 1970

What is meditation? 1998

Why meditation? Delhi, Motilal Banarsidass, 1977

Yoga beyond meditation, 1998

Yoga of silence

The Invincible : magazine published by Vimala Prakashan Trust, (final issue, 2002)